COLLEGE OF SAN MATEO

GATEWAY TO ACHIEVEMENT

1922

CLASS ACT

College of San Mateo
A History

Michael Svanevik & Shirley Burgett

CUSTOM & LIMITED EDITIONS
San Francisco

Initial printing of this book was made possible by a grant from The Foundation for San Mateo County Community College District.

Library of Congress Catalog Number: 96-71234

ISBN (Hardcover) 1-881529-18-5
ISBN (Paperback) 1-881529-19-3

Published by
CUSTOM & LIMITED EDITIONS
San Francisco, California

First Printing

Printed in the United States of America

CLASS ACT

The idea for this book was born during the summer of 1995 when College of San Mateo administrators, faculty and students began focusing on the institution's seventy-fifth anniversary.

A few opposed the idea, arguing that it would be more appropriate to sponsor such a project 25 years from now when the college reaches the century mark.

Obviously, this thinking didn't prevail. A decision was made to go ahead with a book after everyone came to the realization that College of San Mateo will not be able to duplicate this project in the year 2022.

This was a unique opportunity. Authors have been able to talk with students from *each* of the college's graduating classes. Earliest graduates were advanced in age; nevertheless, many enthusiastically shared their college experiences and, in most cases, fond memories of life as it was more than 70 years ago. Early faculty members and administrators who, in a few cases, had been associated with the college as far back as the 1920s, were equally helpful.

College of San Mateo (CSM) already had a long and storied history when it came to occupy its streamlined hilltop campus in 1963. Virtually all of the pioneer educators whose vision and devotion made this new campus a reality, contributed something to the preparation of this book.

Without attempting to be morbid, 25 years from now, when historians set out to assemble a centennial history, almost all of these people will be gone. This was a last chance. The next history, assuming of course that there is one, will be drawn from secondary works.

Students walking south along CSM's main mall toward the library and the physical education complex.

When the authors were invited to undertake this project, they were asked to emphasize students and share with readers what life was like at College of San Mateo throughout the years.

The effort, therefore, has not been to spend a lot of time discussing buildings. But, no institutional survey is possible without some emphasis on the college's various homes which, if nothing else, have been unique.

Readers won't find undue emphasis on administrators, since, with a few notable exceptions, such personalities have been almost invisible.

Allan Brown ('53), longtime professor and dean of students (1969-1992), remembered walking across campus one day with then President David Mertes. Brown paused for a brief conversation with a student. Suddenly realizing that Mertes was also associated with College of San Mateo, the student inquired: "And what is it that you do here?"

Not long after the information gathering process began, one emeritus administrator remarked that he supposed the book would be a "thoroughly sanitized history," implying that in the deep recesses of the college's past, there were injurious secrets which should remain buried.

Perhaps he knew more than the authors have been able to find. In the process of plowing through thousands of pages and chatting with scores of witnesses, they failed to uncover a single juicy scandal *worth writing about*.

There were no terrible tales to tell. No person presently or previously employed by the college asked that any story be altered. If an academic institution is to be evaluated on the basis of behind-the-scenes intrigue or Machiavellian plots, then for 75 years, College of San Mateo has been a notably dull place.

Which is not to say that life at the college hasn't been interesting, unusual and, from time to time, a bit bizarre. Research began in the dusty, cobweb-draped basement of the Administration Building on the College Heights campus where dozens of file drawers and boxes crammed with documents were stored; this was the exciting world before e-mail.

Dating from the early 1920s, documents of every sort were found.

Life for students at College of San Mateo has represented a careful balance between study and play.

They ran the gamut from student records and letters of complaint to presidential correspondence and inter-office memos. There were accreditation reports, personnel records, board of trustee minutes, newspaper accounts of college events, journal notes and even a few long forgotten photographs. To protect student confidentiality, authors steered clear of individual records, academic and otherwise. Everything else in the room was considered fair game.

From time to time, it was found that administrators' comments about faculty members were embarrassingly frank. Other documents were more amusing. Groundsmen in 1963, for example, were asked not to explode dynamite during class hours, something they routinely did to blast holes in the hard ground for the planting of trees.

That relations between faculty and administrators at times showed signs of strain should come as no surprise. Nor is it astonishing that not all faculty has always been superlative.

Whereas over the years, the vast majority of College of San Mateo faculty members have been dedicated and responsible professionals, a few were not. Some abused tenure rights and got away with it. But this is neither a secret nor worth dwelling upon. Any college that has reached the venerable age of seventy-five which hasn't experienced a few such abuses and can't point to a handful of wacky professors, is probably no *real* college.

Finding *all* the documentation to put this book together involved unforeseen difficulties. On the eve of the book's preparation, much of the film archive documenting special events over the years was dumped. An overzealous library employee, when told to get rid of tapes and films not used in three years, took the direction literally and tossed many videotaped records.

Earthquake retro-fitting and repair of the library necessitated that it be vacated in 1995-1996. College archives, separate and apart from the aforementioned materials, were carefully moved to another building for safekeeping. In summer 1996, the authors were asked to identify a photograph found sitting atop a pile of junk in a courtyard outside the cafeteria. Glass broken, the photo was of Charles S. "Jum" Morris, the college's first president. A search turned up other dust-covered archival documents; many were water stained, having been subjected to late spring rains. Discussion with the contractor revealed that these materials had been piled outside the building for weeks. The area was open to anyone who ventured there. The contractor was told that 99 percent of it was garbage.

There was no blame. This was no crime. It was worse. The shabby treatment of the archive was a mistake. Many items were later recovered. A number remained missing.

Class Act is a social history. Some of the more academically oriented readers will be disappointed. It avoids the analytical and is not meant to be scholarly. A few, of course, will then retort that it is mere nostalgia.

The aim is to recall pictures and stories of yesteryear. Many modern readers will likely shake their heads in amazement at the behavior of some college students of the not too distant past.

Students today find it difficult to identify with their counterparts of 75 years ago. Back then, for most, attending classes was their sole responsibility. Today, students don't even know the meaning of the word "frosh." Most have no sense of the difference between "freshmen" and "sophomores" nor that, at least as late as World War II, a blood rivalry existed between members of first and second year classes.

By the 1990s, attending football games was a thing of the past. Years ago, such attendance was virtually mandatory. Those who failed to show up to root for the San Mateo Junior College *Bulldogs*, as students chose to call themselves, faced being ostracized by friends.

Even in the decade after World War II, the college staged elaborate annual homecomings complete with parades, elected queens, and dinner dances. Such events no longer exist.

Today, few remember when College of San Mateo had its last formal dance. No college annual has been published since 1961. For many modern-day students, even the thought of donning medieval caps and gowns and marching in somber graduation ceremonies, once the most revered celebration of the academic year, now seems unimportant and a little silly. Said many students of the 1980s about the ceremony: "It just isn't cool."

Years ago students were, by and large, young, white, single males. Female students constituted a distinct minority. There were neither fees nor tuition. The cost of books and supplies was minimal.

Typical students today are older, frequently members of ethnic minority groups, and there are more women than men, many are married with children. They register for fewer units and are employed more hours.

Even the most supportive College of San Mateo students wouldn't think of chartering a boat or scheduling a train to transport them to Sacramento, Chico or Modesto—as they did in the past—for the purpose of cheering on their team.

Instead, students became concerned about child care, health care and where the money would come from to pay the next tuition bill. The cost of a single textbook often exceeded $50; several hundred dollars a semester for books and supplies was normal.

Faculty priorities have also undergone transformation. In 1933, Carlena Morris, wife of legendary and much beloved President Charles S. Morris, established the Faculty Wives Club, an active organization from its inception.

For the spouse of a new instructor to decline participation was unthinkable. There were monthly meetings in members' homes. The group sponsored teas at Christmas and Easter. In September there was always a formal tea to honor new members of the faculty. But it was more than just tea drinking. Card players belonged to the bridge section. Others engaged in gourmet cooking.

By the early 1970s, however, more and more spouses found it necessary to work. Thus fewer and fewer took part and, after the new chancellor's wife expressed no interest, the organization finally disbanded.

In the 1990s, men's wear for the faculty became increasingly casual. Few wore neckties to class. Even Peter Landsberger, president of the college beginning in fall 1992, while usually a devotee of white shirts and pinstripe suits, frequently attended official meetings casually dressed and without a tie.

Such relaxed attire never would have been seen during the first decades of the college's existence. When Harold F. "Tag" Taggert, history instructor and

Peter J. Landsberger became the college's seventh president in 1992. In an era of reduced budgets, he found creative ways to raise money for necessary projects. In addition to being an educator, Landsberger was an attorney-at-law.

baseball coach beginning in the early 1920s, took to the ballfield with his team, he invariably dressed in a dark suit, starched white shirt, bow tie and fedora.

The town of San Mateo had a population of fewer than 10,000 when the college opened in 1922; the county, a 440-square mile expanse, was sparsely populated with just over 37,000 residents. Today, city numbers exceed 90,000 and the county comprises Northern California's most dynamic community. The college and the community matured together. More importantly, though the history is local, it mirrors a national psyche and ongoing trends; indeed, the college reflects the image of America

Times have changed—dramatically. Things aren't better or worse. But they are different and that's what this book is all about.

When College Heights opened in 1963, it was a showplace among two-year colleges. The straight, clean lines became a photographer's dream. This photograph looked west from the Administration Building toward the Little Theater.

College of San Mateo, since 1963, has occupied a magnificent modern 153-acre, 35-building hilltop campus on a peninsula 20 miles south of San Francisco. Known for expanses of lawn, spouting fountains, reflecting ponds and tree-lined walks, the campus overlooks the tranquil community of San Mateo. The campus is a perfect platform from which to view the 400-square mile bay of San Francisco.

On a line of sight directly east of the campus is a sleek ribbon of concrete, the San Mateo-Hayward Bridge connecting the peninsula with Alameda County. The original 7.1 mile bridge, opened in 1929, was the longest such conduit in the world and the closest automobile crossing to San Francisco. The modern $70 million construction which replaced the original, opened in 1967.

When the air is clear, tall buildings in downtown San Francisco and the majestic silver towers of the San Francisco-Oakland Bay Bridge are easily discernable from the campus.

Not far to the south along the bay marshes, observable from the college heights during the winter season, is a massive mountain of salt dominating the small Port of Redwood City. From there, 300,000 tons of salt are shipped annually. This is one of the four areas of the earth where salt is made by a process of solar evaporation.

Five miles west of the campus, across the low Sierra Morena mountain range, are thousands of rolling acres of lush farms, renowned for Brussels sprouts, artichokes and flourishing floriculture.

Beyond are the jagged steep cliffs, long sandy beaches, rocky shore and crashing surf of the Pacific Ocean assuring that, except on the hottest of days, the college will be refreshed by cooling westerly winds.

Minutes from the campus, nestled at the base of the Sierra Morena, are the Crystal Springs lakes. This sparkling chain of man-made reservoirs dates from the late 19th century. The system was finished in 1890 when German water engineer Hermann Schussler completed Crystal Springs Dam across the neck of San Mateo Creek. For a time, this 154-foot marvel was acknowledged as one of America's first high dams as well as the largest concrete dam in the world.

Today these reservoirs, just one portion of the elaborate Hetch Hetchy system which routes Tuolumne River water 155 miles from Yosemite National Park to the peninsula, continue to be an integral part of the San Francisco Water Department. The system provides all water for the great metropolis and most communities along the peninsula.

Since early in this century, these lakes and adjacent forest land comprising the watershed have been set aside as a state fish and game refuge.

College of San Mateo—so close to civilization and yet so far away. At night, when classes conclude, parking lots empty and fingers of Pacific fog spill silently onto the college's manicured lawns and flower beds. Herds of black-tailed deer, families of raccoons, skunks and occasionally foxes take possession of the campus.

These nocturnal creatures, which invariably vanish into surrounding grassland before the morning light, seem oblivious to the significant role that this particular place continues to play in the lives of the 15,000 men and women who attend classes and to the historic position it has occupied in the social and academic life of San Mateo County.

College Heights overlooks the town of San Mateo and the San Mateo-Hayward Bridge, connecting two counties on opposite sides of the bay.

San Mateo Junior College, as the institution was originally called, was a phenomenon of the early 1920s, a time when educational costs in California were rising. For a student attending a university to pay an annual tuition of $1,000, a staggering sum at that time, was not unusual.

But perhaps worse than the high price of college was the poor quality of education most students could expect. University classrooms were so overcrowded that few were able to provide the academic atmosphere to which students were entitled.

William L. Glascock, principal of San Mateo High School, became an ardent foe of this state-wide problem. He thundered that higher education in California was a "pity," branding it a "shocking state of affairs." He noted that the need for more colleges was so great, and so many young people were being crammed into available classrooms, that first and second year students often didn't get a chance to see the insides of physics and chemistry laboratories but once or twice a year.

Following the lead of the state's top educators, notably University of California President David P. Barrows and Stanford University President Ray Lyman Wilbur, Glascock came out in favor of a *junior college* for San Mateo County.

This unique new institution, he declared, promised potential students opportunities to continue their education while living economically at home. Faculty emphasis would not be writing or research. The goal was teaching excellence with quality classes equivalent to the freshman and sophomore years of a university.

Glascock demonstrated ample precedent. There were already 18 active junior colleges which served almost 3,500 California students.

All along the peninsula, especially in the town of San Mateo, this idea garnered support. San Mateo, a small town which had grown slowly since 1863 when service began along the newly constructed *San Francisco & San Jose Railroad*, was now expanding and leaders were dedicated to further community promotion.

Locally, William L. Glascock was the first major educator to support the junior college idea during the 1920s. His efforts on the luncheon circuit made San Mateans recognize the value of such an institution.

In 1921, backers invested a million dollars in Pacific Studios, a motion picture production facility located along Peninsula Avenue. Movie crews began cranking out feature-length films in an ultimately failing effort to make San Mateo the "Hollywood of Northern California."

Meanwhile, peninsula boosters poured money into yet another grandiose promotional scheme at Coyote Point where builders frantically worked assembling a grand amusement park. Known as Pacific City, this development was soon touted as the "Coney Island of the West" and advertised as possessing California's "greatest bathing beach." Pacific City opened amid much gala celebration, July 1, 1922. It failed within a year.

In this environment, William Glascock took to the luncheon circuit to launch his crusade for a junior college. He found sympathetic listeners for his pitch that "education is the business of the state." He declared also that a college for San Mateo promised education for thousands.

Real estate entrepreneurs were enthusiastic, adding that "there is nothing more appealing to home seekers and others than the knowledge that there are superior school facilities offered in the community." A junior college, said realtors, "will greatly enhance the value of property."

Local chambers of commerce were informed that "better schools mean better business...and better citizenship."

In lock step, one after another, business and fraternal organizations joined the junior college bandwagon. Elsa McGinn, president of the San Mateo Women's Club, summed it up for many when she urged members to support the college. She reminded them that "we are anxious to promote good citizenship."

Opposition to the proposed institution, though an obvious community expense, was almost nil. There seemed to be no question that a community supported junior college was "economically and scientifically" sound.

The few who opposed the college did so on the basis that it was connected to the San Mateo Union High School District, fearing that classes would be taught by high school rather than college teachers, and ultimately would amount to little more than post graduate high school.

Marjorie Brace ('24) was the college's first registered student. "I had in mind to go to Stanford but my folks couldn't afford it...the junior college came along at just the right time; I really don't know exactly what I would have done otherwise."

Voters in San Mateo and Burlingame trooped to the polls March 31, 1922. A junior college was approved by a substantial margin. Glascock called the electoral success a tremendous victory and "a great stride for progressive education."

San Mateo Junior College opened in several rooms of San Mateo High School on Baldwin Avenue at Griffith Avenue (later called San Mateo Drive), Aug. 28, 1922.

The first of ultimately hundreds of thousands to register was Marjorie Brace ('24), a Burlingame girl who had hoped to attend Stanford but had been stopped by high tuition. Brace lived at home and commuted between Burlingame and San Mateo by the electric trolley car.

Even before opening day, Superintendent Glascock, aptly nicknamed "The Boss," deemed his experiment successful. Three students who enrolled were from Lincoln High School in Portland, Oregon; one came from Fremont High in Oakland. In all cases these families had moved to San Mateo exclusively to avail themselves of the new educational opportunities offered on the peninsula. On the first day five students arrived from Redwood City and three from South San Francisco.

San Mateo Junior College, as early faculty used to remark, "found itself nestled in a valley between two mountains of conceit—Stanford and the University of California." Sarcastic though they may have been in reference to the two mammoth learning emporiums, from the beginning, San Mateo was unduly influenced by them.

San Mateo was, to a large degree, a prep school or springboard into both universities. Graduation from the junior college was tantamount to acceptance in either. Students failing to possess the necessary academic credits for university acceptance often spent a year, or as little as a single semester, at San Mateo making up deficiencies. The curriculum was specifically designed in consultation with the universities.

A review of confidential correspondence reveals that, during the first decades, junior college deans and administrators along with the first presidents were chosen by local trustees, but only upon the written recommendation of both universities.

From the outset, scheduling procedures mimicked those of Stanford or the University of California. Opening and closing dates of semesters were predicated on decisions made in Berkeley. Fifty-minute classes, beginning at ten minutes past the hour, were adopted to coincide with the long established U.C. tradition.

A total of 30 students, 18 of them male, comprised the 1922 student body. The number grew to 48 by the end of the school year. "From the day the college opened, the small student body was like a family with everybody having a hand in sports, drama and student government," recalled the late Marjorie Brace.

College students met in the high school cafeteria Sept. 15, 1922, to establish the junior college as an institution entirely separate from the high school. Participants pledged to achieve academic and athletic excellence. Despite the small size of the group, they discussed creating a tennis and football team.

An air of mystery surrounded many early student decisions. The college colors, blue and white, where chosen, according to student Marian Young Erickson, "not for any sentimental reasons," but because students felt that their logical next step would be to Stanford or Cal. "So we took the *white* from Stanford's red and white; the *blue* from Cal's blue and gold."

Student Dorothy Dickie claimed late in her life that the colors were "my fault." She stated that "I had a lot of crepe paper left over from a party. We were planning to give a dance at the college and hadn't much money for decorations, so I offered my blue and white streamers. That settled the problem. *Blue* and *white* it became."

And, whereas pioneer students vaguely recall that the actual color chosen was the royal blue characteristic of the University of California, the actual shade was not official. By the late 1920s, surviving pennants, dinks and other paraphernalia, offer testimony that the colors were *robin's egg blue* and white. Only in March 1928, did students vote to adopt the darker shade.

The precise origin of the bulldog mascot will probably never be known. Legend has it that it was chosen by a process of elimination in that it seemed other schools had commandeered most of the other animals.

Mystery surrounds the choice of the bulldog as the college mascot. Some claimed it was picked because there were no animals which hadn't already been used elsewhere. Others said it was chosen because a local bulldog kennel made a championship English bulldog available for use.

Student Hessie Ballentine, whose parents owned San Mateo's Goldstone Kennels which specialized in raising champion English bulldogs, offered the services of *Rival Goldstone*, "a ferocious animal," to appear at all sporting events. Apparently that proposal settled the discussion. For years, the bulldog, clad in a finely tailored felt coat with matching cap, was a fixture at sport competitions. Many variations of this story can be found.

San Mateo Junior College was the youngest and smallest *jaysee* (as such institutions were called) in California. Thus, its gridiron performance in the first year was perhaps its original unique accomplishment. Of the 18 men enrolled, only four had played football. Undaunted, Coach John Wasley, a high school administrator, glued together an 11-man team. There were no substitutes.

Cheering on "the Dogs" became *de rigueur* during the college's early years. Local newspaper reporters, impressed by the obvious spirit and the "machine-like" qualities of players, termed the "Fighting Bulldogs" the "pluckiest football eleven on the Pacific Coast." The inaugural season will always stand out in the annals of the college as amazing.

Rain or shine, every member of the student body attended games. The San Mateo squad squared off against larger, more experienced opponents. San Jose State Teachers College fell to the Bulldogs in a scrappy contest by a score of 6 to 3. Santa Rosa Junior College crumbled 35-0. In the season finale, the Bulldogs "snapped and clawed" their way to a 33-0 victory over previously undefeated Sacramento Junior College.

In the years before World War II, San Mateo's football prowess was an awesome force to be reckoned with. Part of this success was explained by the fact that potential players bound for either of the two "mountains of conceit," who lacked necessary academic finish for direct admission, were sent to San Mateo for polish. University coaches watched the progress of the home team, which they often called their "farm club."

The college obviously wasn't large enough for athletic specialization. Most football athletes played basketball as well. San Mateo's hoopsters silenced skeptics, vanquishing two of their first three opponents.

Mixing college classes in the same building with the high school was less than ideal. High school enrollment was up and the building was overcrowded. San Mateo was the only high school on the central peninsula. Burlingame High, under construction, didn't open until 1923.

To the dissatisfaction of college students, classes were scheduled at odd hours and late in the afternoons when rooms were available. Superintendent Glascock admitted that he wasn't sure how so many could be accommodated. He predicted that it might become necessary to hold half day sessions with classes scheduled from early morning to late at night.

College social life in the high school setting left many students wanting. Dances were often held in hallways during the lunch hour. "It really didn't seem like we had left high school," wrote Marjorie Brace.

Drama was an important part of college life. On November 17, less than three months after opening, players performed in "Country Cousin." The presentation was in the high school auditorium. Twenty students, two-thirds of the student body, were in the cast. "Such finish and such good taste…like watching professionals in an uptown theater," critics purred. For decades, even after the college moved, the high school auditorium remained the venue for dramatic presentations.

The university influence was omnipresent. In 1923, Ralph Minor, an "examiner" from University of California at Berkeley, inspected San Mateo Junior College. In written comments he lauded the quality, enthusiasm, professionalism and dedication of the new jaysee faculty. Minor, however, was disturbed by the college's lack of a campus, pointing to the desirability of "segregation of…students." He presented Glascock with evidence that "those junior college students who are physically separated from the high school environment have a decided advantage over those who are not."

Drama was an important part of the early curriculum. Students staged a variety of dramatic and vaudeville presentations.

San Mateo Junior College acquired its first independent campus, albeit temporary and makeshift, in 1923, at the beginning of its second year. Classes convened in the former Capt. William Kohl home, situated in the middle of

Between 1923 and 1927 the college occupied the William F. Kohl residence. Vestiges of San Mateo's Gilded Age were still evident. Few who attended there ever forgot its unique characteristics.

16 garden acres, directly in the heart of town. Kohl, a partner in the prestigious Alaska Commercial Company, had made his fortune hunting seals.

The house had been built by Charles B. Polhemus who founded and platted the town of San Mateo in the 1860s. Six years later he sold the home to Peter Donahue, builder of San Francisco's famed Union Iron Works. Occupied briefly by Alexander Austin, a San Francisco official, it was purchased, in 1874, by Kohl.

Kohl enlarged the home significantly and added a Mansard roof. The sprawling estate, marked along El Camino by an elegant concrete and wrought iron fence (still existent), extended from the State Highway to Laurel, and from Fifth to Ninth avenues. In 1921, after a bond election, the property, including the house, was sold to the town of San Mateo for use as a city park (later known as Central Park).

"None of us thought much about the place," admitted Paul Nyeland ('28), a creator and art editor of *The San Mateo Centaur*, a humor magazine considered risqué by the college administration. "There were a whole flock of big old houses around here."

Innovative thinking was required to transform the three-story, 13-room white Victorian, located roughly at Fifth and Laurel avenues, into anything resembling a functional academic institution.

Students, who began classes there Sept. 4, 1923, discovered enduring traces of grandeur indicating that in its heyday when San Mateo was still widely known for its luxurious estates and fine society, this house must have been magnificent; it still dripped of tarnished elegance, though Kohl had died in 1904 and his son Charles Frederick had vacated the home in 1914.

While it was true that they creaked, floors were hardwood parquet, fashioned from black walnut and white mahogany put together with brass nails. In high-ceilinged rooms, illumination was provided by crystal chandeliers with dangling prisms. These sparkling baubles soon disappeared into pockets of souvenir-seeking students. No one denied that the chandeliers offered touches of class to the decaying building, but the illumination provided, while dramatic, was far from adequate. Walls were covered with brocade hangings rather than paint or wallpaper. Ornate fireplaces were in every room.

San Mateo Junior College's entire student body sat for a photograph on the steps of the Kohl mansion in 1924. Slicked down hair, shoes and neckties testify that 1920s students were swell dressers.

Workers enclosed the once broad veranda, creating a library separated from the rest of the house with a Dutch door. Students weren't allowed to browse the stacks. The grand dining room became the assembly hall and site of college dances. Chairs were simply pushed aside.

During the college's later years at the mansion, after repeated requests from students for a store of their own, in 1926 the wine cellar was transformed into a co-op (where scholastic supplies, pennants, Bulldog stickers, sophomore paddles, chocolate and other basic necessities were purchased). "Classes were held in the parlors and bedrooms," stated Franklyn "Jeff" Lyons ('26). Students recited Shakespeare and studied astronomy in a quaint upstairs sitting room still decorated with delicate satin-tapestried walls.

Bulldog Dorothy Fowler ('26), a sophomore class officer, reminisced about folk dancing in the kitchen, learning English and history in the dining room and biology in a bedroom. Kohl's once sumptuous study was the physics laboratory. Lush grass surrounding the house was particularly vivid in Fowler's memory. "During physical education, we often played soccer on the lawns." Ventilation was poor; on warm days most classes were held in the gardens.

Physical education instructor Leonora Brem noted that workers erected a platform out in the park where women could engage in calisthenics.

Pioneer student Dorothy Dickie entertained fascinated listeners with stories about how she'd learned French in the master bedroom. She always smiled when noting that the plumbing in the adjacent all-marble bathroom was defective and gurgled when water was used anywhere in the house. Such inopportune, unscheduled and, at times, unpleasant interruptions caused considerable faculty annoyance, but were always a welcomed occasion for levity among distraction-seeking students.

Frank M. Stanger, who joined the faculty as a history instructor in 1928, wrote in the college's twenty-fifth anniversary keepsake booklet, that the cavernous Kohl kitchen was transformed into the women's locker room and gymnasium. Men's physical education classes were always scheduled at nearby San Mateo High School. Closets and one-time bathrooms were used as faculty offices.

If a conclusion can be reached by numbers alone, San Mateo Junior College was a roaring success from the start. When classes began in the Kohl mansion there was an enrollment of 50. By the end of 1923, the number had risen to 80. The following fall, there were 137.

By the third year, two temporary buildings leased from the city were erected in the park and a couple of tents, for use as classrooms, were put up on the grounds. Student Jean Williamson ('29) remembered the unheated, damp and drafty tents which leaked when it rained. One, in which she took speech, was especially unpleasant during winter months.

Until 1935, San Mateo was the sole junior college on the peninsula. Nor was there a junior college in the East Bay. Many commuted from San Francisco and North San Mateo County by streetcar, *Car 40* as most called it, or aboard Southern Pacific commuter trains.

The drafty, swaying streetcars, which sped down the peninsula at tremendous speed, were always teeming with students, some bound for San Mateo High School as well. Beginning with its first year, San Mateo was commonly known as a "trolley car college." Eleanor Fourie ('35), who commuted from

South San Francisco, related that while most of her friends took the trolley, the huge electric monsters made her "seasick." She came by train.

Late in the 1920s, San Mateo was the college of choice for 40 East Bay students. Most lived in boarding houses or with local families. Ten commuted daily. School officials calculated that these students were spending four hours per day on streetcars and ferryboats. Thus, in 20 class days, each was losing 80 hours, or more than three full days. The rigors of this commute were significantly lessened in March 1929 with the opening of the San Mateo-Hayward Bridge.

Local students seemed inordinately impressed by what they considered the sophistication and cosmopolitan air of those who came from San Francisco. Many even smoked. Eugenia (Jean Cloud) Reynolds ('26), an especially vivacious young woman from San Jose, found city students awkwardly cliquish. "Especially the groups from Lowell really stuck together."

One San Franciscan, Robert Levin, who attended for a single semester in 1927, vividly recalled the agony of his daily commute. It required transferring from one streetcar to another in the city before boarding a train at Third and Townsend. For him, this ritual consumed between two and three hours. Finally, Levin convinced his father to buy him a car.

Likewise, students from as far south as San Jose came via train. Groups boarded at Mountain View, Palo Alto and all stops along the route. Hitchhikers, thumbs extended, dotted the State Highway (El Camino Real) both north and south of San Mateo. Harry Gray ('26) remembers that "drivers were very good about picking up students."

Some out of town students rented rooms in San Mateo. There were a number of downtown boarding houses. Perhaps the most fashionable was the old Christian de Guigné estate home located near the college. De Guigné had been the son-in-law of San Francisco banker John Parrott. The boarding house sat in the middle of wooded property extending from El Camino Real to San Mateo Drive, and from Third to Fourth avenues. This grand old home was destroyed in 1927 to make way for construction of the Benjamin Franklin Hotel.

The jaysee attracted students from all over the Bay Area. Locals claimed that those who came from San Francisco brought with them an air of sophistication.

STUDENT ACTIVITIES

17

No African American in San Mateo was more popular than Noah Williams. He opened a cafeteria on B Street in 1920. So successful was it that in 1925 he created Noah's Ark one of the first businesses on Third Avenue. Students received discounts and flocked to Noah's to enjoy his Southern cuisine.

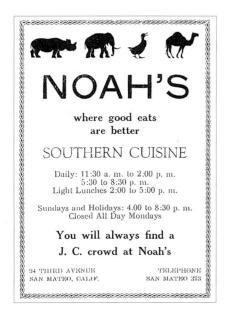

An antique house was a poor substitute for a real school. At the Kohl mansion, there were neither lockers nor places for students to study or comfortably congregate between classes. Some lounged on the grand stairway with its beautiful mahogany banisters. Others clustered on lawns or jammed into nearby parked cars.

The opening of San Mateo Junior College coincided with the beginning of the Jazz Age. In September 1924, some students solved the problem of what to do during tedious hours between classes. Music became the popular diversion. All they needed was a portable phonograph, a few jazz records and a shady spot under the big palm tree near the house.

No food service was provided at the college. Students brought their own, went home to eat or gathered in groups to lunch in town. Noah's Cafeteria, "where good eats are better," was perhaps the eatery of choice on B Street (late in the decade, the restaurant was renamed Noah's Ark and moved to Third Avenue).

It was run by Noah Williams, San Mateo's best known African American, who had previously worked as a railroad chef. Famed for Southern cuisine, notably Virginia baked ham and fried chicken, he provided 50 percent discounts for students. Williams faithfully advertised in college publications, informing readers: "You will always find a jaysee crowd at Noah's."

French Club members usually followed popular instructor Dorothy Herrington to Chartiers (later Villa Chartiers), a small restaurant on El Camino Real at East Santa Inez. In addition to taking continental nourishment—a full meal for 35 cents—Miss Herrington attempted to stimulate conversation in French. "And my, did they chatter," sparkled Herrington in an interview decades later. "Topics like the weather were discussed earnestly." Chartiers was the scene of numerous comic French skits and monologues. French folk songs and the *Marseillaise* were sung with "great gusto and much rolling of the r's." By the beginning of the 1930s, the French Club, or *Le Cercle Français*, had a prestigious reputation as one of the oldest organizations in the junior college.

Creameries on B Street offered toasted sandwiches and milk shakes or ice cream sodas for a quarter. An extra thick shake, by itself, sold for a dime.

With uniformity, members of the student body during the college's first decade agreed that attending San Mateo Junior College was something of a magical experience. Emmet Hayes ('30), one-time editor of *The San Matean*, often reflected on the San Mateo years. "I never had a better time in my life. Although there were relatively few students, they were a great bunch of friendly people and the instructors were excellent."

Administrative leadership during the 1920s, was provided by Superintendent William Glascock and on campus by Robert J."Hoppy" Hopkins. Formerly on the faculty at the University of California and hired upon that institution's solid recommendation, the be-spectacled "Hoppy" was assigned to teach physics at both Burlingame and San Mateo high schools in addition to serving as dean of the junior college. Former students remember Hopkins as pleasant and occasionally strict but not much of a leader.

Academically, San Mateo freshmen stacked up well vis-a-vis other jay-see students in the state. In 1924, a few more than half who took the Subject A examination (Bonehead English) managed to pass. Statewide, the average was 44 percent failure. Of 160 at San Mateo who took the exam in 1925, 84 passed.

Eugenia (Jean Cloud) Reynolds was struck by the youth of the faculty which "didn't seem much older than we were." Nevertheless instructors always maintained a professional decorum. Students were consistently referred to as "men and women" and addressed by their last names preceded by the appropriate miss or mister. "It all made us feel very adult."

Throughout the 1920s, women consistently wore pullovers with Peter Pan collars, pleated mid-calf skirts and socks with brown and white saddle shoes. Men commonly wore tweed knickers along with Oxfords or two-tone saddle shoes and high socks. Cardigan sweaters, often with neckties, were especially stylish. Three-piece suits didn't attract special attention. Shirt collars were stiffly starched. Hair was slicked back. Looking swell and sophisticated was a characteristic of the 1920s.

San Mateo Junior College was an especially good place for a woman to be during the 1920s, added Eugenia Reynolds. During her concluding semester,

Robert J. Hopkins, the first dean, was not distinguished for his leadership. The former physics professor attempted to maintain San Mateo's prep school character. But, when other views prevailed, Hopkins left the college in 1931.

"there were 150 boys and 50 girls." Not long after graduation, Reynolds married fellow student Roy N. Cloud.

Until the end of academic year 1927, the Kohl mansion remained the center of college life. The dining room or assembly hall was the venue for both barn dances and more formal dances to honor entering freshmen. After 1927, when the luxurious Benjamin Franklin Hotel opened on Third Avenue, formal dances were held there. Most considered the hotel's facilities ultimately sophisticated and elegant. But now and then, particularly grand functions were held at the Belmont Country Club.

While those who attended college in the house often wax nostalgic about its one-time splendor, most didn't fully appreciate it while there. Space was always cramped. The *Bark*, as the student newspaper, a weekly, four-page, four-column publication first published in September 1924, was originally called, referred to the mansion as a "funny looking...dilapidated old house."

Doors had to be kept closed on cold days and an inadequate furnace couldn't keep the place warm. When the furnace did work, it blew hot air and made so much noise frustrated instructors often turned it off. Then students froze. Gas pipes leaked and, more than once, escaping fumes forced evacuation of the building. Art students complained that light in their so-called studio was so dim that they were forced to carry flashlights on dark and rainy days. Effective lighting was long delayed.

Bark writers faithfully recorded the school's deficiencies. Editors reported that the place "resounded" with the clicking of a *single* typewriter. When the overworked machine ceased to function in 1924, it was considered important enough to report it in the town newspaper.

Almost simultaneously, installation of the college's first telephone caused much student glee. Many agreed that its "now and then ringing" alleviated "utter boredom." Faculty, on the other hand, grumbled that the annoying sound reverberated through all the rooms of the house, interrupting their lectures.

Despite the unorthodox surroundings, students worked valiantly to maintain outward appearances that theirs was a *real* college and thus mimicked the shenanigans typical of prestigious universities.

After the first year, fervent competition grew up between first and second year students. During the initiation period of several weeks, entering women were required to wear jeans, plaid shirts and non-matching socks. Make-up and nail polish were both strictly forbidden. Traditionally, green hair ribbons were to be worn until an official Associated Women Students' tea.

Likewise, men wore jeans with non-matching socks. Shoelaces were to be untied. They were required to wear the traditional blue cap or "dink" acquired at the student store. "I remember being forced to make a fool of myself together with other new enrollees by marching down the street, pant legs rolled up and singing off key," stated Harry Gray, elected president of the freshman class in 1925.

Each first year male was required to carry a decorated wooden paddle which was frequently and strenuously applied to his rear end by sophomore men for any of a dozen real or imagined infractions.

Freshmen, arriving the first day, were treated to a "paddle party—a warm welcome that they will remember for a *long* time." This was meant—literally.

Incoming freshmen were expected to take beatings and paddlings "like gentlemen." Harsh treatment of new students became a proud tradition during the college's early years.

Hazing was "brutal." Recalling the dedication with which sophomores applied themselves to this principle, Paul Lorton ('29), a lifetime college booster, stated that "during hell week, sophomores beat the hell out of us."

Physical hazing gradually became San Mateo Junior College's most historic tradition and one in which students who endured it took enormous pride. Freshmen, told to accept the hazing "like gentlemen," were subjected to vigorous beatings with belts, boards, paddles and fists. Not infrequently, a few wound up in Mills Hospital. Punishment by paddling, "to be carried out by the sophomore and high freshman classes en masse," was the sentence for any infraction.

Cigarette smoking, regarded by men and women of the 1920s as a rite of passage from high school to college and thereafter seemingly an inalienable right, was completely forbidden to *all* students anywhere around the dilapidated house, but was permitted in other parts of town. Frosh women were allowed to smoke if they humiliated themselves by using cigarette holders. Men were permitted to smoke corncob pipes only.

Student Joe Catanich ('26) felt compelled to codify the rules. These were initially published Aug. 19, 1924. Thereafter, even when the campus moved in academic year 1927-1928, *Freshmen Rules* were conscientiously printed, unchanged, in the student handbook.

Wearing the "dink" was absolutely required at all times. Gardens on the north side of the building were termed "the sophomore lawn." No freshman dared tread there. The designated "upperclass bench" was sacred to sophomores. Though the bench's precise location was never clearly revealed, freshmen found lounging there were treated with utmost severity.

"Queening," a practice defined as becoming "unduly familiar" with college women, was denied incoming male students. "Unduly familiar" meant carrying on any conversation with a woman for longer than *one* minute.

Attending college meetings—11 a.m. until noon on Friday—was, without exception, a freshman's duty. Wearing belts, insignia or emblems from other schools or colleges was strictly forbidden. Freshmen were allowed to park their automobiles on Fifth Avenue; *never* on Laurel. Freshmen males were *never* allowed to wear knickers, a special privilege coveted by upperclassmen.

Bark editors warned that freshmen persisting in violation of these afore-mentioned rules would not only be paddled unmercifully, they would also be impressed by the "toe of a thick-soled boot." Thus, they concluded: "A word to the wise is sufficient, so take heed Frosh!"

Women freshmen deemed guilty, however capriciously, of rule infractions were forced to endure "incongruities of costume" so that the "criminals" would be easily identifiable. They were required to wear their clothes inside out. Some were humiliated by having to recite the alphabet backwards during the Friday college hour. Others were sentenced to memorize nursery rhymes and recite them on demand by upperclassmen.

A knowledge of the college hymn, *Hail, San Mateo*, written by star base-ball and football player Jerry Nyhan in 1924, was mandatory. Most Bulldogs sang the words to the first line and insisted on humming the rest. Freshman didn't get away with such nonsense. Many dutifully pasted the words in their dinks, realizing they might be asked to sing it at anytime.

Academically, San Mateo Junior College toed the line. Faculty members, it appears, felt an avowed responsibility to build the school's reputation by carving a place for the young institution on the academic map.

Jean Williamson reported that she felt the quality of teaching was excel-lent. "The junior college experience worked really well for me. I went on to the University of California and was far better prepared for what was required of me than had I gone directly from high school…besides it was easier to get in as a junior." Paul Lorton who went from San Mateo to Stanford, was equal-ly positive about his jaysee years. "We were thoroughly prepared at San Mateo Junior College for the academic obstacles we were expected to deal with."

Both Williamson and Lorton spoke glowingly of the skills and dedication of numerous pioneer faculty members, especially Ada Beverage, a one-of-a-kind woman who, over the years, taught drama, public speaking and English.

Another of the revered pioneers was the fabled Harold F. Taggert. Hired in 1923 as an instructor of history and social science, Taggert came to San Mateo after assignments at Santa Maria Junior College and a university in the East. He was acclaimed for his unique sense of humor and his multifaceted

Social scientist Harold Taggert was acclaimed for his articles which appeared in scholarly journals. He also served as a dean, coach and later director of instruction. He started at San Mateo in 1922, and led the academic procession at the dedication of the new campus in 1963.

personality. For years, besides teaching, he wrote historical articles for scholarly journals and coached the baseball team.

William Glascock, in 1922, could not have foreseen the rapid growth of the junior college. Students seemed to materialize out of nowhere. The following fall there were an amazing 137 students and, by 1924, the freshman class alone was bulging with 102. College officials noted that even with temporary buildings and a couple of tents, the maximum that could be accommodated was 400. That number, 125 of whom were women, was reached in 1926.

The breaking point came in fall that year when a record 250 freshmen were accepted. They brought the student body, along with 180 returning students, to an unbelievable 430. Ninety-eight unhappy applicants were turned away.

Spring, 1927, was the last semester the college convened in the old house. San Mateo High had also outgrown its Baldwin Avenue property. A new high school facility, on grounds along Delaware, east of the railroad tracks, long under construction, was now ready for occupancy.

Thus, Baldwin became San Mateo Junior College as of July 1, 1927. When classes began in September, the student body had grown to 480. Of this figure, 325 were men; there were 155 women. The Kohl home had seen hard service. Though a few in the city wanted to see the place transformed into a recreation center, it was destroyed in 1928.

Acquiring a "genuine campus" was cause for considerable enthusiasm experienced by both faculty and students. "The full-sized college building creates an attitude of dignity among the students," declared Frank Haley, the student body president.

Students saw the move to Baldwin as the beginning of a new, more modern era. Barely had classes convened for the inaugural semester when Dean Hopkins canceled them on Friday, Sept. 16, 1927, to afford everyone an opportunity to visit muddy Mills Field (San Francisco's

The college took over a small portion of San Mateo High School on Baldwin Avenue for a year in 1922 and acquired the whole building in 1927. Baldwin served until 1955 when it was taken over by the U.S. Naval Reserve. Ultimately, it was wrecked to make way for the Mills Medical Arts Building.

new municipal airport) to watch the landing of aviation hero Charles Lindbergh in his legendary *Spirit of St. Louis.*

Griping was an integral part of college life. Bulldogs growled about fellows who refused to buy student body cards but drove around in fancy roadsters, daily eight o'clock classes, mentholated cigarettes and afternoon laboratory sessions.

Without doubt, the most enduring dissatisfaction was brought about by the absolutely no smoking rule: "Lady Nicotine is not allowed on campus." Many felt abused that they weren't allowed to puff away on the broad front steps of the college. They lamented that "students of the University of California are allowed to smoke on campus. Why can't we?" (State law forbade smoking on the grounds of any state institution with the exception of the University of California where its board of regents was responsible for creating the rules.)

The edge of campus property to the east, near San Mateo Drive, was marked by a footbridge over San Mateo Creek. Rain or shine, addicted students and faculty members crowded there between classes and at lunch time to smoke. Perhaps more communication went on there between faculty and students—certainly more than took place in faculty offices—than at any other place on the campus. Aptly, this viaduct was soon known, and for decades referred to, as *Nicotine Bridge.*

Instructor Dorothy Herrington enjoyed reminiscing about academic life at Baldwin where she found faculty meetings especially delightful. The small group was so closely knit and "we always stayed for coffee and cookies afterward." Instructors were required to sign in daily, noting the hour of their arrival, at the college office.

San Franciscan Bob Levin commuted by streetcar and train. So many hours were consumed, he finally convinced his father to purchase this 1927 Jordan Playboy 8 Roadster. Commute time was cut significantly.

Appearance of *The San Mateo Centaur,* a 16-page independent publication owned and run by San Mateo Junior College students, came in 1927. It was edited by Jack Patterson ('28) and Ted Kaplanis ('28). The publication's motto was "It's All in Fun" and "Death to Gloom."

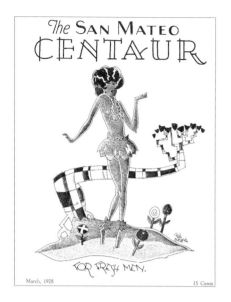

The San Mateo Centaur, *a comedy magazine for "Fresh Men," was introduced by students in 1927. Though administrators disavowed it, the high quality of the short-lived humor magazine was a source of pride.*

From the moment it first appeared in October, *The Centaur* was a point of campus pride. Much of the clever and suggestive cartooning work was done by art editor Paul Nyeland.

Advertised by editors as a "vest-pocket edition" of the Stanford *Chaparral* and the University of California *Pelican*, it was the first humorous magazine ever printed in an American junior college. While enthused and impressed by the publication, Dean Hopkins felt compelled to tell local reporters that it was not an authorized college publication. Students who owned the magazine were required to excise the name San Mateo Junior College from its masthead.

The highly successful magazine, the logo of which was a centaur reaching for an apple from a naked (but neither offensive nor overly bodacious—indeed the ideal figure of the 1920s) Eve, sold on newsstands and bookstores in Berkeley and from San Francisco to Palo Alto. Aimed at "Fresh Men," the quality was such that it soon sold at selected colleges across the nation.

The first issue consisted of spicy stories, jokes, poems and cartoons. In no sense of the word was it a literary magazine; it was devoted to humor.

Administrators and student body officers objected to the fact that the official junior college newspaper had been called *The Bark*. Perhaps they felt that the name was trivial and lacked the dignity they believed this official journal deserved. Thus, upon movement of the campus back to Baldwin, the newspaper was changed to *The San Matean*. The first edition under the new masthead was Sept. 7, 1928. *The San Matean*, originally a sophisticated, eight-column full-sized newspaper, was published bi-weekly. The new journal was often touted as "the most professional of all junior college publications."

Classes were held exclusively at Baldwin for eight years. But in some ways the aging high school facility wasn't a tremendous improvement over the old house. The library, an academic center set aside for quiet and study on any campus, was situated in a low-ceilinged room with creaking floors directly beneath the school's auditorium.

Although librarian Katherine Steele pleaded with students to maintain silence, the place was always plagued with noise problems. Study in the library was virtually impossible. Heavy walking overhead echoed throughout the library.

COLLEGE HUMOR OF THE '20s & '30s

"Is your Mother away now?"
"Yes, she's gone to Baghdad."
"Really, I didn't know he got away."
The Bark, Oct. 28, 1924

HARRY: "Who was Hamlet?"
JOE: "Your ignorance is refreshing. Bring me the Bible and I'll show you."
The Campus, 1924

HE: "I had a nightmare last night."
SHE: "Yes, I saw you with her."
Centaur, October 1927

JOE: "I am taking up the study of illumination."
JANET: "Oh? Light reading."
Centaur, October 1927

HE: "There seems to be something wrong with the motor."
GIRL OF THE MOMENT: "Don't be so foolish; wait 'til we get off the main road."
Centaur, December 1927

She was only a taxidermist's daughter, but she knew her stuff.
Centaur, March 1928

CITY DUDE: "This sure is a one-horse town."
STREET SWEEPER: "You wouldn't say that if you had my job."
Centaur, March 1928

BETTY: "My dad's a doctor. I can be sick for nothing."
FRED: "That nothing. My dad's a preacher and I can be good for nothing."
The Campus, 1930

HINTS TO GRADUATES: The stork is the bird with the longest bill.
The Campus, 1931

SHE: "What's the matter Alex?"
HE: "I wrote an article on fresh milk and Art condensed it."
The Campus, 1931

And there is the one about the Scotchman who married a tattooed dancer so his children could see motion pictures.
The Campus, 1931

COP: "Who was driving when you hit that car?"
DRUNK *(triumphantly)*: "None of us; we were all in the back seat."
The Campus, 1933

Heard on the air:

TEACHER: "Johnny, how do you spell necking?"
JOHNNY: "K-N-E-C-K-I-N-G"
TEACHER: "That's wrong!"
JOHNNY: "Yeah, I know, but it's lots of fun."
The San Matean, Sept. 21, 1933

Blaring trumpets and drums beating during orchestra classes and the harmonious sounds of two glee clubs which met in the auditorium continually shattered the sanctity of the academic hall. (The Music Department was added in 1928.) Alleviating the noise was a goal the college never achieved. In one attempt, administrators ordered that Miss Steele's office be surrounded with glass barriers to muffle the "annoying incessant clicking of her typewriter."

One room was set aside for the comfort of women students. Equipment therein included chairs and card tables for bridge games, all the rage during the era. This accommodation, however, caused male Bulldogs to growl. "Such, with the addition of ashtrays and free cigars, would be very handy for the men." An editorial in *The San Matean* noted that commuting students needed some sort of lounging room where they could assemble and talk. "The cars parked in front of the campus form a very incomplete clubroom." It was pointed out that their "lecture-wearied attention" would be attracted by the acquisition of a pool table. Deans weren't amused.

Students at the Baldwin campus complained that there was no place to congregate between classes. Many crowded into cars. Some played bridge on the lawn under the palm trees.

In fact there was virtually no place for students, commuters or otherwise, to congregate. Janet Munro Boyer ('38) recalled that her friends passed time between classes crammed into parked cars or sat around on automobile fenders—if they had any. "That's where we learned to smoke." Some students took advantage of friendly people who lived in the vicinity to study in their front yards.

Eleanore Nettle added that many students gathered on the front lawn, under the palm tree, to play bridge. This activity was thoroughly frowned upon by student leaders who believed that card players created the public impression that the jaysee wasn't the academic institution it claimed to be. College rules condemned card playing on campus and student editors railed against the bridge groups. Nevertheless, the games went on.

Bridge was in, but by 1930, tennis was considered king on the San Mateo campus. Everybody played with everybody anytime they could find a racket and a court.

"I had a really good time in college," stated Janet Boyer. "As far as I was concerned it was a great party school. We were always having hayrides near the

Peanut Farm in Woodside and barn dances replete with blue jeans, old cords, corn-cob pipes and ginghams." Typically held at the Devonshire or Belle Monti country clubs, the barnyard atmosphere was created by a precarious buggy and assorted farm implements. There were also a lot of dances in the college gymnasium on Second Avenue. "Afterward we'd walk over to the Oak Tree Inn on Third Avenue (just east of El Camino Real) to drink beer…we may have been underage but the authorities always looked the other way."

Exciting, expanding San Mateo, where the ever-increasing population edged past 10,000 by the end of the 1920s, took enormous pride in being a college town. There was much delight that this prestigious institution of higher learning was directly in the center of the community. Downtown San Mateo was dotted with boarding houses occupied by out-of-town, primarily male students. (Women students frequently rented rooms with individual families.) There was no doubt that the college contributed to the community's prosperity.

Restaurants and other businesses rolled out welcome mats, hoping to attract students. Entrepreneurial sorts clamored to buy advertising in college publications. Riteway Sweet Shop, across the street from Baldwin, offered Bulldogs' special rates and boasted it was "where the Jaysee has breakfast."

Pantages Candy Shop, at 144 B Street, featured a toasted sandwich and extra thick milk shake for a quarter. The carefully contrived advertisement read: "Cynical, canny, connoisseurs, continually congregate to consume contentedly their luncheon at *Pantages Candy Shop*, comprehending completely that this cognomen conveys courtesy, candidness, cleanliness and congeniality."

In 1928, the Booterie, on B Street, offered women students shoes in the latest styles, patent, kid or satin heels, for $7.50. Men's tan Oxfords sold for $6.50. Robert W. Gates of Burlingame opened its "College Shop" and advertised "collegiate tailor-made clothes and exclusive apparel" for college men who considered themselves "swell dressers." Morse Pharmacy, at 100 B Street, noted that it was the "nearest drug store to the college."

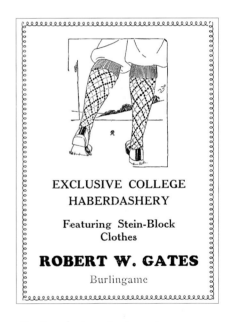

EXCLUSIVE COLLEGE HABERDASHERY

Featuring Stein-Block Clothes

ROBERT W. GATES

Burlingame

During the jaysee's pioneering years, local entrepreneurs competed for the best positioning in college publications.

Stanford and the University of California boasted "most beautiful women" and "most popular men contests." Not to be outdone, Bulldogs created a tradition of their own—*Whiskerino*, a twice yearly contest to locate the student who could grow the longest, most luxurious beard in two weeks. They took the opportunity to show college women that "a hairy chest is not the half of it." Beards were solemnly judged by a distinguished faculty committee. Local merchants showered the college with prizes for the most striking beards. The grand prize was a semester free-pass to the New San Mateo Theater.

Bob Jacobi, proprietor of Bob's Barber Shop at 309 Second Avenue, a regular advertiser in *The San Matean*, reserved the right to cut the winning beard—with an especially fancy razor donated by Pope's Drug Store.

The distinctive Benjamin Franklin Hotel, San Mateo's only highrise, became the site of semi-annual teas for women students and other elegant college convocations. Often as many as 200 women faculty and students, clad smartly in gaily-colored afternoon gowns, crowded into the main lobby of the hotel to sip tea and munch watercress sandwiches.

Faculty leaders feared that by 1936, proper etiquette and the art of genteel tea drinking was becoming lost. That year, before the spring tea, Mildred Brown Robbins, society editor of the *San Francisco Chronicle*, was invited to campus for a special "women students only" convocation to discuss rules of etiquette which she declared were "as old as the history of the race."

Several years after the onset of the Depression, college teas were moved from the Benjamin Franklin to the parish room of St. Matthew's Episcopal Church. The cost of such an afternoon, a burden to many students, was reduced from 35 to 15 cents; afternoon gowns were replaced by less formal day-to-day school clothing.

By promising reduced rates, Benjamin Franklin Hotel managers enticed students to play miniature golf on their 27-hole course opposite the hotel.

Owners of the New San Mateo Theater which opened on Third Avenue in 1925, and later the Baywood Theater which began operation on B Street in 1931, offered auditoriums free of charge, for college assemblies and lectures.

In 1929, two years after the college moved into Baldwin, the nation's economy plummeted. A growing economic depression, characterized by rising unemployment, stimulated enrollments as never before. For some, the jaysee offered a vehicle in which to ride out the crisis; for others it was a place to acquire new and usable skills.

Almost immediately the campus became too small. "Temporary" buildings, "shacks," soon made permanent, were erected on the grounds. Closets, sheds, any place where students and teachers could assemble, were transformed into classroom space. The library was hopelessly inadequate. Classes were held wherever there was enough space to cram bodies.

James R. Tormey Sr., who joined the faculty in 1933 to teach English and public speaking, recalled Baldwin's uncomfortably crowded conditions. He taught classes not only on campus but in a room borrowed from a Methodist church in east San Mateo. His other classes met at Froebel Hall, an abandoned kindergarten on Ellsworth. Now and then, Tormey was scheduled into the Central Grammar School, a dilapidated relic located across the street from the campus. By 1935, Baldwin was bulging to the breaking point. School officials were trying to cram 1,500 students into a building built for 500.

Upon the return to Baldwin, Claude Petty, editor of *The San Matean*, noted that there "is not much danger of doing too much studying in San Mateo." Petty continued, stating that "the courses here are easier than at the University of California, because the instructor does more work. The student gets a fact drummed into his mind until he knows it." Berkeley professors required students to search for hidden facts that they "seldom make clear."

"The success of San Mateo Junior College was its dedicated, hard-nosed faculty," stated Edward Bauer Jr. ('30), later publisher and editor of the *Half Moon Bay Review*. Bauer believed that engineering at San Mateo was perhaps superior to any such department in California.

But the Depression and economic necessity pushed this proud principle of high quality, personalized education, at least temporarily onto a back shelf. Facilities were hopelessly overcrowded. Tormey's public speaking classes were often crammed with up to 50 students. If participants had the opportunity to stand and speak two or three times a semester, Tormey considered the class successful.

Throughout its first decade, San Mateo Junior College was conceived of solely as an academic institution. Indeed, many continued to regard it as a prep school for Stanford and Berkeley. Dean Robert Hopkins was still at the helm when the first breezes of academic revolution, already blowing elsewhere in California, were felt in San Mateo.

By 1930, there was a growing feeling that junior college programs needed more flexibility and greater responsiveness to requirements of the entire community. Educators had a responsibility to recognize needs of all citizens, young and old, not simply those few bound for prestigious universities.

This movement, representing a radical change in the philosophy of junior colleges, was spearheaded in 1931 by the Seventeenth District Congress (San Mateo County) of the Parents and Teachers Association along with the local chapter of the American Association of University Women.

As a rule, students themselves did not take well to these whispered rumors of change. They were aroused by what they perceived as an effort to lower standards and dilute the academic reputation of the junior college. They expressed fear that adoption of anything but purely academic courses would contribute to their college becoming the laughing stock of the peninsula. Many threatened a walkout unless some unified program was created. Much of their ire was directed against the feckless dean, Robert Hopkins.

Hopkins and virtually all of the faculty dug in their heels, determined to prevent what they felt would be the ultimate decay and destruction of a fine academic institution. Again rumors spread that the board intended to replace Hopkins if he did not fall into line with the new thinking. Instructors, en masse, signed a petition threatening resignation if Hopkins were replaced or if San Mateo's coveted academic programs, which they had laboriously created, were diluted.

Wisely, school board members waited until just after graduation in June 1931, before showing Hopkins the door. Whether he walked through it or was shoved is unclear. In any case, he was out. His "resignation" was quietly and quickly accepted. A half dozen instructors immediately resigned. Many, perhaps because of the Depression and financial commitments, did not.

However, it appears that some of this group never overcame their bitterness and spent the remainder of their careers in opposition to the college's redesigned goals. After 1931, San Mateo was well on the road to becoming a "community" rather than merely a "junior" college.

San Mateo trustees launched a serious search for a new dean. As usual, queries were sent to the California Teachers Association, Stanford and the University of California. A single recommendation was received from the three. He was Charles Shoemaker Morris, dean of Modesto Junior College.

Morris, born (1887) in Southern California, was the son of a high school principal father and a mother who had also been a teacher. He attended Stanford where he came under the philosophical sway of the brilliant progressive educator-president David Starr Jordan, a man who had long been an ardent supporter of the junior college idea. Morris graduated in 1908. In addition to academic accolades, he left Stanford with an athletic reputation as a top cinder man.

Sometimes likened in appearance to boyish-looking aviator Charles Lindbergh, the imposing Morris was six feet-four inches in height and proportionately well developed. His weight hovered around 200 pounds.

While at Stanford, he was familiarly known as "Jumbo" or "Jum" a nickname which stuck with him throughout life. In later years, after he had achieved both a state and national reputation as an educator who ardently advocated junior colleges, many did not even know his name was actually Charles. During his early years at San Mateo, messages to students which appeared in college publications were invariably signed "Charles S. Morris;" later messages were simply signed "Jum."

From 1909 to 1915, he coached athletics at Palo Alto High School while assisting with the track program at Stanford. After 1915, he accepted the position of vice principal of Modesto High School.

Charles S. "Jum" Morris came from Modesto Junior College to become dean at San Mateo in 1931. Six years later, trustees named him San Mateo's first president. More than any individual, Morris blazed the trail toward the modern community college.

Modesto Junior College opened in 1921; Morris was appointed its first dean. Six years later, with the creation of the position of president, Jum Morris was named to that position. During his tenure at Modesto, that jaysee rose from a school with a mere handful of students to one of the leading junior colleges in the state.

While he was reluctant to leave Modesto (and indignant students there protested his defection), a higher salary, greater personal administrative control and more attractive weather enticed him to San Mateo as dean in 1931. He was given the title of president and superintendent of the college district in 1937.

Until his death in 1952, Jum Morris became San Mateo Junior College's best known symbol. Historian Frank Stanger wrote that he was the "guiding spirit of the institution." Well liked even by those who opposed some of his professional views, Morris was exceedingly popular with faculty and students. Many recall his omnipresent, cheerful face towering above the crowds at sports events, slapping old-time football players on the back while reminiscing about historic passes and end runs.

Jum Morris made the college function smoothly. He did what needed to be done. There are always apocryphal stories associated with such personalities. With uniformity, those who remember the Baldwin years tell of the day a new young faculty member got off the streetcar and walked up the front stairs to meet with Jum Morris. He encountered a man, broom in hand, sweeping the steps and asked directions. The broom handler, taken for a custodian, was Morris himself.

Morris' broad concept of the junior college reflected the progressive thinking of David Starr Jordan and other forward-looking leaders of the junior college movement. For Morris, a jaysee represented more than the first two years of university work.

Essentially, Morris felt the strength of America rested in the junior college. "In its development lies the answer to the quest for equal opportunity for all." He called upon citizens of all ages to participate in the system.

He became known as one of California's most eminent educational statesmen. "Adult education at San Mateo Junior College is an expression of the basic philosophy of this school and is particularly significant in that it demonstrates that adults, no less than the youth of a community, need and utilize educational facilities when they are made available to them in convenient and usable form."

Those faculty members willing to give Morris' ideas a chance became the new dean's ardent admirers. During his tenure at San Mateo, more and more faculty emphasis was placed on assisting students who would not proceed beyond the junior college. Nevertheless, his supporters adamantly defended him, noting that his move toward broadened college goals in no way diluted his dedication to San Mateo's traditional academic purposes.

He declared that jaysee instructors should be a unique breed, better prepared in subject matter than high school teachers and better teachers than most university professors. "The Ph.D. degree of the college professor is a mark of attainment in research, a primary function of the university, just as the teaching credential is the measure for capacity in instruction, the primary function of the junior college." The time and energy of the junior college teacher belongs in the field of instruction.

Student Eleanore Druehl Nettle ('33), commenting on the overall cooperative nature of the faculty, believed that at San Mateo Morris achieved his goal. "As a rule," stated Nettle, "instructors were tough, but by the time students were through, they were really prepared to go on."

Nettle admitted that at Baldwin, the facility was less than ideal. The swimming team worked out at Harding Pool, "an awful place," across Second Avenue. Students paid $1.25 a month for the privilege. Nettle noted that "the pool water was thick with green moss."

Even before the arrival of Jum Morris, San Mateo Junior College had acquired a reputation for the overall quality of instruction. One of the more outstanding was Fred Klyver, instructor of biological sciences.

Klyver achieved worldwide recognition among biologists. Not only was he responsible for discovering a new form of algae in California's Huntington Lake, he wrote a book on *chermindae*—jumping plant lice.

Student Francis D. Wyatt ('29) was especially taken by Klyver's scientific brilliance but, he admits, apparently not enough to regularly attend laboratory classes.

Wyatt vividly recalled the day Klyver suggested that, as a result of absences, the errant student might well not pass the course.

There was one way to save himself. Klyver was doing an experiment involving wood ticks and needed specimens. Wyatt volunteered to find them. He ran through high grassy fields with his shirt off, collecting a dozen healthy ticks. Klyver removed them with gasoline. Wyatt passed biology.

Depression years were pivotal in the college's history. The rapidly rising enrollments between 1927 and 1935 demonstrated just how thoroughly inadequate the Baldwin campus actually was. Homer Martin, district superintendent, toured the building and declared that it was in "terrible condition." He estimated that the cost to bring it up to any kind of standard would be $75,000 to $100,000. And even then, the place would be inadequate.

The college took its first step toward building a new campus in 1935. Thirty acres, on the northern edge of San Mateo High School at Peninsula Avenue and Delaware Street, were purchased at a cost of $67,500. Martin announced that it was the most far-reaching action taken by the school board in a decade. Martin declared that the new campus was ideally situated for students of both Burlingame and San Mateo. For others, there was easy access by trolley, train and bus.

During the 1930s, trustees began building a new campus on Delaware at Peninsula Avenue. This effort was short circuited by World War II and never resumed. Nevertheless, from 1939 to 1963, San Mateo students took science and mathematics at the Delaware campus.

Elaborate plans for the new campus, a cluster of streamlined buildings in a "modernized classical style" not unlike a Roman city, were meticulously drawn by supervising architect George W. Kelham. They showed a junior college of unrivaled beauty fronting on Peninsula Avenue.

Before long the college began construction of a $350,000 science building, the first unit at this new site. The new building was heralded as the most important event of the decade for the college. It was completed and classes commenced there in 1939. This inaugurated a protracted era of dual campuses. Almost all mathematics and sciences classes were scheduled at the Delaware site. Throughout the day, students migrated between campuses. They hitchhiked, bicycled and strolled. Two bright yellow buses were rented from the high school to shuttle them back and forth. One bus left each campus at precisely two minutes after the hour.

From the outset, the building proved to be something of an embarrassment; it was built two feet shorter than its plans. County Superintendent of Schools James Tormey, later commented that "the carpenters measured from one end and the plumbers measured from the other, and some pipes were four feet out of place."

Despite its rough edges and, in some ways, primitive facilities, international students especially found a cosmopolitan air and comfortable environment in which to learn at San Mateo during the 1930s.

State statistics published in 1935 indicate that there were 134 foreign born members of the student body. San Mateo was bettered only by the University of California with 582, the University of Southern California with 249 and the University of California, Los Angeles with 209. If percentages rather than actual numbers had been provided, San Mateo's position would have been significantly higher.

The local institution was jolted in February 1935, when it was learned that San Francisco, which had no campus of its own, planned to open a junior college in the fall. When it did, San Mateo enrollment immediately fell from

A school bus left Baldwin and Delaware each hour to shunt students between campuses. Later, when a third campus at Coyote Point was added, the shuttle service went between all three.

Beginning with its earliest years, the campus was a haven for international students. In the 1960s, Registrar Herbert Warne developed minimum academic standards in English for those seeking admission. By 1989, there were 130 students from outside the United States representing 36 foreign countries. By 1991, 171 foreign students were enrolled from 38 different countries.

1,600 to 1,000. San Mateo lost both students and many thousands in tuition monies paid by the City and County of San Francisco.

The dramatic decline in enrollment necessitated trimming faculty. Some junior members were cut from full to half time. French instructor Dorothy Herrington suddenly also found herself assigned to the physical education department, teaching badminton and archery.

And, when the college economy didn't immediately resurge, Jum Morris suggested that Herrington create a new class—in "homemaking." Apparently quite popular, the course included minute training on how to make beds with hospital corners.

Beginning in 1924, a college yearbook, *The Campus* was published annually. Though selling it was always time-consuming and difficult, it had a reputation of being a well-planned, classy presentation. *The Campus* was particularly posh in 1928, lavishly illustrated and hard-covered, measuring 9 by 12 inches.

In 1933, with the Depression and curtailment of a variety of funds upon which the students had previously counted, a number of activities were canceled. The first inclination was to cease publication of *The Campus* because some felt it was non-essential. But upon reconsideration, student editors followed the lead of Franklin D. Roosevelt and trimmed back the frills. Price of the bare bones book was slashed from several dollars to a mere 50 cents, the lowest since the college had opened. The "Depression-sized," 32-page, six- by nine-inch yearbook was distributed in May 1933. Though vastly reduced in size, it still contained all the essential elements, albeit abbreviated, which had appeared in previous editions.

Likewise, *The San Matean*, a large 17-inch by 22-inch format before the economic crisis, was now halved to "depression size." Editors claimed they'd overcome "all obstacles."

One day, during the heart of the Depression, Jum Morris went home for lunch. He was concerned, he told his wife, Carlena, that it appeared that some boys were going to drop out of school because they had no place to live.

"My mother got to thinking that they might rent a house and set up a cooperative," stated Betty Morris Roehr ('32), daughter of the president.

The college's Mothers Club supported the idea and the *San Mateo Times* solicited donations from the public. Keeping students in college became a community effort. Townsfolk came forth with beds, furniture, linens and all kinds of other necessities.

The first dormitory, for 12 boys, opened in a big old house on Feb. 15, 1938. Located at 517 San Mateo Drive, the house rented for $30 a month. A second house, with accommodations for 14, opened Sept. 9, 1938, near the Delaware campus at 15 Dwight Way in Burlingame. Each house had a single bathroom.

"In the beginning both places were in pretty bad condition," recalled Roehr. They needed painting and a lot of fixing up. Everybody— many people who had nothing to do with the college—pitched in.

"Dorm Boys," as residents came to be known, paid a munificent $7.50 per month. Included in the price was a clean bed and a responsibility to keep the place clean and take care of gardens.

Wholesome meals were part of the plan but food wasn't included in the price. "We ate well," declared Bill Quinn, "It cost us about 35 cents per person a day."

Carlena Morris, the "official" house mother, took her responsibility very seriously. She didn't want "my boys" eating out of cans. They were expected to sit down for dinner. She prepared the menus. "For a while my mother did a lot of cooking…creating recipes. Then she would take the food down to the dorms. If the boys liked the meals, they could cook them themselves after that." Cooking responsibilities were rotated.

"Ma" Morris, as the Dorm Boys called her, considered the dormitories a grand success where "26 boys clean their own houses, cook their own food and wash their own necks without supervision or instruction."

Which did not mean she didn't keep a close eye on what was going on. Every boy on his birthday received a home-baked cake with candles. Thanksgiving and Christmas, for those who couldn't go home, mothers

When Jum Morris and his wife realized that some students would have to leave the college because of financial setbacks during the Depression, they opened two dormitories in old houses (1938), one near the Baldwin campus and one (pictured) near Delaware. They were run under the watchful eye of the Mothers Club.

brought turkey dinners. During the holiday season, the Mothers Club provided Christmas trees complete with lights and ornaments.

Without fail, every Sunday evening Charles and Carlena Morris visited each dorm. "Visits weren't really inspections," reported Quinn. Although, he admitted, Ma usually went upstairs to check that everything was in order. Betty Morris Roehr stated that her parents were "genuinely fond" of the Dorm Boys. "They would sit around the living rooms and chat."

After the first not so gentle breezes of academic reform swept through San Mateo early in the decade and the subsequent appointment of Jum Morris, changes came slowly. A number of special classes were adopted for adults. One of the first was aeronautics.

Responding to requests from the public, a novel approach in itself, Morris, in January 1932, approved a vocational course covering the theory of flight, aerodynamics, navigation, meteorology and air traffic law. Aeronautics, scheduled to be taught at Curtiss-Wright Field in San Mateo, filled almost immediately.

Other new classes almost crept into the schedules. One course in parliamentary law, designed for the Parent Teacher Association, was taught under the auspices of the junior college at Sequoia High School in Redwood City. Another group of classes was designed for the County Nurses Association.

Finally, in 1936, with almost no pre-planning, Morris appointed instructor James R. Tormey Sr. to establish an Adult Center associated with the college. He was given two weeks to design a curriculum, acquire a faculty and advertise the program. These were to be evening classes offered on the Baldwin campus.

Morris had expected that not more than a handful would partake initially. But between 200 and 300 adults signed up the first night of registration; by the end of the first week, the number had risen to 500. The adult program, which dramatically altered the character of the college, proved to be an unmitigated success. By the end of the academic year 1943, there were 5,073 enrolled.

MA & THE DORM BOYS

Throughout World War II, letters by the hundreds came to the home of Jum and Carlena Morris. Most began simply and in the same way: "Dear Ma…"

"I haven't a darn thing to say and don't even know where I am," began a scribbled note from Donald Rude, "I just thought I'd say hi."

Another soldier wrote from somewhere in Europe: "Those good cakes you used to make would sure hit the spot right now…do you remember the birthday parties and the Sunday night feeds we had? I didn't realize what a great life I had when I was back home…"

Bill Quinn ('42), a member of an Army regimental combat team in the Philippines, told Ma: "I've had my fill of bananas."

"Ma" was Carlena Morris, wife of President Jum Morris. During the Depression, when continued enrollment of some students was threatened, she became the force behind the creation of two dormitories, one in San Mateo and one in Burlingame.

Dorm Boys became her extended family. For those who went overseas, she assumed the role of faithful correspondent. On birthdays, she sent cards with neatly typed original poems. She mailed copies of The San Matean by the hundreds. Often she sent class schedules with notations about courses.

There was always a Christmas card including addresses of all Dorm Boys. Jum and Carlena often had snapshots taken which she faithfully enclosed with her correspondence.

"She sent the same kind of newsy letters I got from my own mother," said Bill Quinn. "I often got as many as two chatty letters a month from her…she was quite a lady, just a mother."

Dorm Boys responded in kind. She was showered with letters, cards, invitations to weddings and, later, baby announcements. News-hungry servicemen asked about friends or inquired about the successes of the Bulldog football team.

During the war, as enrollment dwindled, the dormitories closed. "I was sorry to hear 517 San Mateo Drive got closed up," wrote Pvt. Stanley Soult. "I often think of the swell times I had while I was there. I sometimes wonder what I would have done if it had not been for my being able to get in there when I did."

Morris' unique relationship continued beyond the war. Correspondence was maintained. As late as the 1970s, she sent out addresses of all known Dorm Boys and requested recipients update them. Former Dorm Boys brought families to visit.

Carlena lived until 1987, dying at the age of 99.

Between the establishment of San Mateo Junior College in 1922 and World War II when varsity sports programs were temporarily suspended (1942-1945), the institution became feared and respected as one of the athletic giants of Northern California. In many sports, even four-year institutions were forced to bow to San Mateo's might.

Beginning in 1923, when he was hired to coach and teach physical education, the name Murius McFadden became synonymous with sports at San Mateo. "Mac," a native of the Northwest, and graduate of Oregon Agricultural College in Corvallis, was well versed in all phases of sport and never failed to develop teams of high caliber. During his long career, until retirement as College of San Mateo Athletic Director in 1964, he was often called the "mentor of the Bulldogs" and the "Matean Maestro." His years as choreographer of the football team brought him his greatest glory, but, for a time, he coached basketball and track as well.

McFadden unlocked the doors of the Bulldog kennel and led the Dogs to their first California Coast Conference Championship in football in 1925.

The Bulldogs, acting as a smoothly oiled powerful machine, won every conference game. There was pandemonium in the streets of San Mateo after the local boys rolled over San Jose State Teachers College by an impressive 44 to 13 score. Jubilation reigned in the last game of the season when the Bulldogs pawed their way to a 7 to 6 victory over Chico.

The following year, not having lost a football game to a jaysee team in three consecutive years, San Mateo traveled to Southern California to play Pasadena for a Thanksgiving Day classic, the Junior College Championship of California.

Twenty-two players and coaches boarded the S.S. *Harvard*, an overnight steamer to Los Angeles. But the ship sailed into the eye of a Pacific storm and all aboard became seasick, causing players to arrive weak and wobbly. Heavy rains before the game kept the "Macmen" from exercising stiff muscles and joints. On game day, the skies were bright and the Bulldog defensive game was dazzling, but in their weakened state they were unable to withstand a fourth quarter thrust by the Pasadena Pirates and fell in a 7 to 6 defeat. Spirits dampened, McFadden and his team had their Thanksgiving feast in Pasadena.

Murius McFadden (right) became football coach during the early 1920s. His teams dominated jaysee football. During his long career he coached basketball and track as well. Later he became Athletic Director, a position he maintained until 1964, a year after College Heights opened.

McFadden's well-oiled gridiron machines dominated jaysee football for years. Championships were won in 1925 and again in 1928 when San Mateo won 10 consecutive games. The team took second place in the conference in 1924 and 1926.

During the college's first decade, the opponent for the annual Big Game on Thanksgiving weekend was Chico. However, by the 1930s, the Thanksgiving matchup and concluding contest of the season was against Sacramento. This was always a major event, accompanied by appropriately noisy ballyhoo.

Ray Daba ('35) recounted amazing tales of 1934 when the Bulldogs, the strongest team ever fielded at Baldwin, smashed their way to the state championship by ripping through San Francisco State, Stanford, St. Mary's, Marin, the University of California, Santa Rosa and Modesto.

The Big Game that year was played in Sacramento. A paddle wheeled riverboat was chartered to carry several hundred enthusiastic rooters on the overnight cruise. "There was a bit of drinking aboard," Daba admitted. "Nobody slept all night. Most students didn't have cabins except those who were especially affluent or who had planned to do special entertaining." Late in his career, McFadden admitted that the tradition of going to the Sacramento game by riverboat had to be stopped after the year 1935 when San Mateo students almost destroyed the boat.

By the time the team took to the field they were pretty exhausted. Nevertheless, the "Goddess of Fortune" shone on Bulldogs. The stubborn and determined Sacramento Panthers led at the half, but the Blue and White came away triumphant with a 14 to 6 victory.

Albert Bigley ('35), also aboard for the Big Game, has no recollection of the outcome. "Most of us didn't get to the game but stayed aboard the boat and slept." Daba added: "Coming back, we were a pretty dull group." Still, a Thanksgiving feast for the college rooters was provided afloat as well as a "Victory Breakfast" before coming ashore the next morning in San Francisco.

During the 1920s, San Mateo's greatest football match-up was the Thanksgiving game against Chico. A decade later, leagues were reshuffled and the Big Game was with Sacramento. Rooters chartered the overnight steamboat for the trip up the river. Ultimately, this tradition was halted because of damage caused by over enthusiastic college participants.

The riverboat tradition fell by the wayside in 1935. The "ancient, time-worn" means of getting to the game by boat was replaced by a chartered train. Southern Pacific added special cars, with seats removed to facilitate dancing.

Customarily, San Mateo's Big Game was preceded by the "Bulldog Rally" to spur the local lads to victory. Held at the campus, first at San Mateo Park and later at Baldwin, the pep rally featured a bonfire and the entire yell leading squad armed with appropriate cheers. Not just students but the entire town was invited. Both college dean and town mayor were usually in attendance.

Participating with the cheerleading staff was considered an honor and a duty. Freshmen who didn't memorize songs, yells and chants were severely punished.

The first such extravaganza, when the fire was built 12 feet in diameter and flames easily rose 40 feet, was staged in 1924. A full-grown bulldog, symbolic of the team's fighting spirit, made his appearance to demonstrate to all "just how vicious such an animal really is." Handbills promised that "the mysterious legend" of this wonderful dog would be disclosed to all those present at the rally.

"Bigger and better" became the annual slogan of the Pep and Rally Committee. Over decades, intricately planned bonfires progressed in sophistication until they achieved genuine magnificence. Responsibility for these giant pyres was placed in the hands of engineering students who regarded their assignment with a great deal of seriousness.

Southern Pacific could always be counted on to provide railroad ties for the base of the fires. In a few cases, as many as 500 were used. Determined to have the biggest bonfire in the "long history" of the school, the Pep and Rally Committee, in 1927, collected burnable materials for weeks. The fire, it promised, would be over 50 feet high.

In addition to Southern Pacific's contribution, they pridefully gathered 70 barrels of sawdust, hundreds of boxes, old furniture and several decaying stagecoaches which had outlived their usefulness. San Mateo and Burlingame merchants delivered mountains of cardboard and wooden boxes, so many it seems, that by the night of the bonfire, not a single box could be found in either town. Telephone poles and cans of crude oil were added to the pile.

It seemed the entire town gathered at Baldwin on the cold night of Nov. 22, 1927. Blazing timbers cast a warm glow over the massive crowd. Flames shot skyward and sparks showered the downtown area for blocks around. Students with garden hoses and fire extinguishers protected surrounding property. The fire blazed throughout the night.

Until the late 1970s when environmental concerns ended the bonfire tradition, constructing the fire (a process often requiring weeks), and then preventing it from being prematurely torched by opponents of the college, were solemn responsibilities no San Matean took lightly. Even the town's police chief, Thomas Burke, provided uniformed officers to assure that the rally and fire took place as scheduled.

It was great to be a Bulldog in academic year 1928-1929. In the college sports annals, few years stand out so vividly. Those who played varsity sports that year were lovingly termed the "Twenty-Niners" and bathed in the "golden rays of victory." San Mateo athletes seemed absolutely invincible. Between fall 1928 and June of 1929, five teams brought home championships.

Coach and mathematics instructor Sam Francis, an immigrant from Britain, made the name 'soccer' a synonym for victory. In fall 1928, his kickers bested the University of California varsity and humbled Stanford's on the road to winning a third consecutive Intercollegiate Peninsula Soccer Championship.

Francis' teams continued their winning ways. In 1930 the team captured a fifth consecutive title. This was especially amazing in that the league included three, four-year institutions. Soccer competition between Stanford and San Mateo Junior College was the most bitterly contested athletic event of the decade. Not until 1932 did the Indians of Stanford finally manage to lick the Bulldogs of San Mateo, taking their hides and what was next dearest to them—the Intercollegiate Championship. Ironically, the victorious Stanford squad was comprised chiefly of San Mateo graduates.

Murius McFadden's footballers in 1929 won the California Coast Conference Crown and his basketball varsity won the Northern and Central Junior College Championship. In track and field McFadden's men chalked up San Mateo's first cinder victory.

Imitation of Stanford's bonfire became a tradition which lasted until the 1970s. Fires were intricately planned and executed. Southern Pacific traditionally provided most of the fuel.

Until he went off for service in the Navy, 1943-1945, "Furious Murius," as many delighted in calling McFadden, was the darling of the San Mateo campus. His was among the most frequently printed photographs in *The San Matean.* In 1940, students dedicated the college annual to him.

In the spring of that same exciting 1929, San Mateo's baseball squad, coached by Dean of Men Harold F. Taggert, tasted success in nine out of ten outings. At Modesto the Bulldog Varsity Nine grabbed the California Coast Conference Crown. Baseball, as a varsity sport, dated from 1927; this was the first championship in the college history. (In an awesome display of talent, San Mateo's "Tagmen" won 22 out of 27 games in 1933.)

San Mateo athletes continued their winning ways in 1929 when enthusiastic Eli "Sy" Bashor, a Harvard graduate who taught history and civics and who had coached tennis since the college adopted the sport in 1926, choreographed San Mateo's netmen to a winning season, capturing the All-State Junior College Tennis title.

San Mateo's athletic teams were known for their prowess. In their most amazing year, 1929, Bulldogs won state championships in football, basketball, baseball, track and tennis.

Athletic dominance continued throughout much of the 1930s. Championship titles seemed to come in bunches. In 1934, San Mateans won in track and field, tennis, crew, basketball and golf.

Dean Jum Morris hired Oliver E. Byrd in 1932 to teach biology, health and physical education. Morris then asked Byrd to coach track and field, a challenge the young instructor enthusiastically accepted.

Only then did Byrd learn the difficulties. There was no track to run on, no equipment to work with and, worst, no athletes eager to form a team. He could find no safe area for throwing a discus or javelin and no place to pole vault, high jump or broad jump. "In short," stated Byrd, "we needed everything. So we started with what we had and built from there."

Results were phenomenal. During the five years he coached, 138 men signed up for track and field. These athletes set 16 national and world records at the college level. Five individual team members qualified for the New York City preliminaries for the Berlin Olympic games of 1936, only one ended up at the U.S. national team.

Archie Williams, an extraordinary African-American sprinter who had gone on to the University of California, ran in Berlin. At San Mateo, Williams had lost only one race in the 440 yards in about 20 contests. Running for the American team in Berlin, Williams won the Gold Medal in the 400 meter sprint. He joined runner Jesse Owens in ruining Adolf Hitler's day and the Olympics in which the German leader had hoped to showcase the superiority of Aryan athletes.

Student Archie Williams, who commuted to San Mateo from Oakland, set records in track and field. In 1936, after transferring to the University of California, Williams ran in the Berlin Olympic Games and captured a Gold Medal.

"You might not have heard anything about it yet, frosh, but you're going to wear dinks; you're going to be hazed; you're not going to walk on the sophomore lawn, and there are a lot of other things you're not going to do but you are going to like it," began an editorial in *The San Matean* in 1930.

So-called freshmen rules were rigidly enforced by a Sophomore Vigilance Committee comprised primarily of athletes, members of the coveted Varsity "S." The committee did not permit cringing, ducking or hiding. Freshmen who failed to "take it like men" were treated especially harshly. However, Varsity "S" leaders boasted that in only a few bad cases were freshmen knaves sent to Mills Hospital.

By the time Jum Morris became dean, this diabolical sport of sophomores was regarded by students and faculty alike as the college's longest standing and, many felt, proudest rituals. "It is the only tradition that has originated with and survived through the development of our junior college." Although as early as 1930, Dean Robert Hopkins, following the serious injury of a student hit with a belt buckle, had attacked the notorious ceremonies and attempted to curtail excesses. He had met with little success.

Morris, who first faced the student body in fall 1931, demanded that the grim and rigorous practices end. He pointed out that freshmen got nothing from the process except bruised bodies and a whole-hearted hatred for the college's upperclassmen. Unlike the feckless Hopkins, Morris meant business.

Stunned, sophomores groaned. They lamented the passing of this "innocent" tradition, nostalgically recalling the "good old days." Morris, they declared, was being unfair because "a few members of the sophomore class" overstepped the bounds of common sense. They reminisced about when "hazing was a pleasure and not a crime" while bemoaning the fact that now they weren't even allowed to "have revenge."

Whereas the imposition of Sophomore Rules, including the wearing of blue dinks or green ribbons and general humiliation of freshmen continued, hitting with belts, hands, boards or anything else that was handy, ceased. Beginning in fall 1931, direct personal combat between upper and lower classmen was restricted to a single day, *The Brawl*.

This unique event, dating from the early 1920s, held semi-annually on the college field, became famed in the annals of San Mateo. Faithfully attended by townsfolk and student body alike, the Brawl, organized violence, was a mammoth mud orgy including specific events such as jousting, three-legged basketball (with boxing gloves), a sack fight, and ended with a tug of war in which one team—usually the freshmen—was dragged into a pit of swirling mud. The teams, lustily cheered by spectators in a setting not unlike Romans

Hazing of freshmen often resulted in injuries. Wood paddles, vigorous use of which often raised vicious blisters on the backsides and legs of participants, were sold in the college bookstore. Not uncommonly, some who were injured ended up in Mills Hospital.

and Christians, squawked and fought. Laughing was interspersed with howls of pain and fright. Participants frequently required medical attention.

By the late 1920s, San Mateo Brawls had received wide acclaim, far beyond the borders of the town. On February 19, 1928, Fox Movietone News arrived in San Mateo "to get the dirt," on this unusual event, recording it for the weekly newsreel. Recording the Brawl on "talking film" was a first. The next month students had a night out at the Peninsula Theater in Burlingame to watch themselves on the silver screen. There wasn't an empty seat in the house. Editors of *The San Matean* boasted that, as a result of the newsreel coverage, the college achieved fame from "Miami to Nome."

During and after 1931, when physical hazing was finally eliminated, Brawls acquired added significance. Only the toughest participated in the "annihilation" of the opposition. Sophs were coached by Murius McFadden. Harold Taggert offered pointers to freshmen. Usually with more than 1,000 sneering, chanting spectators in attendance, lowerclassmen took to the field sore because they'd been forced to bow down to the mighty sophomores. Upperclassmen were determined to break the "cocksure attitudes" of the lowly frosh.

This 11 o'clock matchup was followed by a gentlemanly "free lunch" in the gymnasium. All bearers of student body cards were invited to participate in a major feed of "pork, ice cream, beans, milk, rolls and cookies."

During the Morris years, physical hazing was replaced by a freshman-sophomore competition known as the Brawl. Held each semester, the Brawl always featured a major bout of mud wrestling on the field at Baldwin.

At the Baldwin campus, Monday, Dec. 8, 1941, the day after the Japanese bombed Pearl Harbor, student body president Clifford Pierce ('42) remembered shocked students milling around, buzzing about what had happened. There was an assembly in the auditorium. Jum Morris and Pierce spoke to the gathered students briefly. President Roosevelt's declaration of war was broadcast to all students. "There was total and absolute silence in the hall," recalled Pierce. "I think we all realized that our lives would be changed forever."

In the days that followed, students began to disappear. "We all kind of lost interest in school. Our classes no longer seemed to mean very much," continued Pierce who dropped out in February 1942. Briefly he worked in an electronics plant in Belmont on a top secret project called radar. "I didn't even know what it was supposed to do." Within a few months, he'd enlisted in the Navy and had begun training to become an aircraft carrier pilot.

Actually, unbeknownst to most on campus, San Mateo Junior College had become an active participant in World War II well before the official American declaration. In that the nation officially maintained its neutrality, college contributions were disguised as "defense programs."

Most were classified. Instructors began teaching classes for the U.S. Coast Guard and for employees of United Airlines at the airport. The government felt "there was no time to waste." New instructional equipment was purchased by the college and sent to the airport. Classes were scheduled 22 hours per day, six days a week.

In early 1943, after American entry into the war, students living in the dormitory at 15 Dwight Way in Burlingame were evicted to make way for others, civilians—at least they didn't wear uniforms—the U.S. Army Signal Corps sent to San Mateo to receive training in the use of radar.

Instructor John Hecomovich teaching on the Delaware campus. Along with Jacob Wiens, he developed courses in electronics. During World War II, the two men were involved with the government, secretly developing courses in radar. Later, they took part in the development of the atomic bomb.

San Mateo's was one of the top such programs in the state of California. The only other technical course in radar was offered at Stanford University. Those involved in this training received instruction every day except Sunday. If a holiday came in the middle of a week, it made no difference; classes were held.

Two college instructors, Dr. Jacob Wiens, an electronics marvel, and John Hecomovich, were instrumental in developing the program. With flimsy excuses, in 1943, both men left the employ of the college, much to the dissatisfaction of Signal Corps officials who relied heavily upon their expertise. Hecomovich was sent to do development in electronics at Oakridge, Tennessee. (He returned to San Mateo after the war to teach electronics and, for a time during the 1960s, served as chairman of the Technology Division.)

Wiens, in 1943, announced he was resuming pre-war efforts at the University of California. He allegedly spent the war years working on the transmutation of gold into mercury. (Wiens also returned to San Mateo at the war's end and was instrumental in building KCSM-TV, one of the first college television stations in California.)

Only after their return to San Mateo was it learned that both men had been secretly involved in designing electronics for the Manhattan Project, participating in the development of the atomic bomb.

Electronics wizard Jacob Wiens (second from left) personally built frequency modulation equipment and arranged for KCSM-FM to broadcast from the Baldwin campus during the 1950s. After the move to College Heights, he became the father of KCSM-TV which began broadcasting in 1964. Wiens is pictured with Station Manager Douglas Montgomery (left) and Chief Engineer Joe Morgan.

Only sweat and blisters will keep the wolf from America's door, said Agriculture Department officials early in World War II. The increased demands for food, to feed expanded armies and citizens in occupied lands, would almost certainly result in major shortages. Governmental officials predicted that by winter of 1943, unless citizens provided for themselves, there might well be food riots throughout the land. 'Victory Gardens,' they announced, could solve the crisis.

Californians took the warnings seriously. By March 1943, an estimated half million people in the state were tilling backyard plots or partaking in larger community projects. Many, who'd never pulled a weed or staked a bean, were digging, planting and cultivating.

In San Mateo, the college assumed the initiative for encouraging patriotic agriculture along the Peninsula. Jum Morris, who immediately designated 12 unused acres of the Delaware campus as a Victory Garden, appointed botany instructor Fred Klyver, whose association with the college dated from 1927, to spearhead the effort.

Klyver was viewed as a master organizer. His new title was Victory Garden Supervisor. "If America is going to feed the world in the coming months," declared Supervisor Klyver, "Joe and Jane Citizen must help feed themselves." Klyver was so successful in encouraging participation that San Mateo County became one of the top producing regions in the state.

The local citizenry was invited to take part in the project. Each received a small plot of land. The college furnished water without charge. "All citizens have to supply is seeds and the effort." By spring 1943, students, faculty and local residents were busily at work planting 450, 20 by 40-foot plots.

PROFESSOR CREATES LASTING INSTITUTION

In 1943, when workmen in Millbrae uncovered a mammoth tooth, they called San Mateo Junior College and asked for historian Frank Stanger. So established was his reputation as a scholar, even with the proximity of top paleontologists at Stanford and the University of California, it seemed the appropriate thing to do.

Stanger excavated one of the most significant prehistoric discoveries ever made on the Pacific Coast. Found were elephant bones, tusks, teeth and other specimens including a tooth from a prehistoric horse. Inquiries from scholarly institutions flooded the college.

Stanger, who died in 1980, left his mark on San Mateo County. "I always kind of had an urge to study local history," he said in 1971. "I just…had the feeling that local history could be interesting and important." He started a county history class at the college.

An historical organization formed in 1935 "to preserve relics, historical data and information about San Mateo County." Stanger was elected president of the group in 1937. After 1942, he served as executive director.

"I felt a growing urge to establish a museum," reported Stanger. He took the idea to Jum Morris. Trustees subsequently gave the college-associated museum enthusiastic approval. It opened on the Baldwin campus Jan. 29, 1941.

There were barely enough documents, relics and materials to fill it.

Stanger became a master collector. "Things hitherto considered unworthy of notice due to their lowly nature came out of trunk and attic."

By 1943, Stanger's museum was a recognized resource for teachers of local history. He was the only man ever to hold the title "San Mateo County Historian."

When the college prepared the move to the hilltop, Julio Bortolazzo and the trustees were unanimous in their "full concurrence" that the museum should remain a part of the institution. Agreement was reached for construction of a $100,000 museum, half to be paid by the college and half by the county.

The long life of the San Mateo County Historical Museum is attributable to Stanger's organizing skill and the marriage he arranged between the museum and College of San Mateo.

However, budget cutting of the 1980s combined with new state laws requiring the college to change for use of campus buildings, made it necessary for the college to re-evaluate this relationship. This, along with the museum's desire for more space, forced the institution to find a new facility. A dissolution of the college-museum relationship will undoubtedly occur before the turn of the century.

Those who participated long remembered a Hillsborough matron, mistress of one of that elegant town's grand estates, who arrived daily at Delaware to work on her Victory Garden—in a chauffeur-driven limousine. The chauffeur always stayed, not to assist his employer in her work, but to cultivate his own plot.

Many potential gardeners were disappointed when they were unable to acquire a plot. So successful was his effort that Klyver acquired permission to begin planting on another 10-acre piece of land in east San Mateo where Sunnybrae School was later built.

Throughout the war, gardening courses, scheduled by the college, were always full. Participants crammed classrooms at Baldwin and Delaware, flowed into the hallways and down the stairs. Instructors also taught in community locations from San Bruno to East Palo Alto.

Klyver wrote a weekly article for the *San Mateo Times*. Topics ran the gamut from where to buy seeds and soil preparation, to planting techniques and when to harvest. His successful teaching methods brought rewards. Mr. J.A. Briggs of Burlingame planted eight pounds of potatoes on the public dump east of town. He harvested 250 pounds.

Anson Burleigh, who learned to start his own plants from seed, harvested 60 pounds of yams from a single row. Waving stands of corn growing on Klyver's plots near Sunnybrae averaged 11 feet high and rivaled the most majestic plants grown in Iowa.

A federally assisted canning center opened in San Mateo in summer of 1943. Citizens were asked to provide their own produce, jars and lids. Thermometers, pressure cookers and other equipment were furnished at no charge.

San Mateo Junior College trustees approved funds for a Community Canning Center on college property in 1944. An entire building, one of the 'temporary' structures built in the 1920s as classrooms on the Baldwin campus, was set aside for the purpose.

The college's center opened in June under the supervision of the California Bureau of Canneries. It was run by a certified inspector-teacher. The center broke all California wartime canning records. Fifty thousand cans of meat, vegetables

Botany instructor Fred Klyver (left) was appointed San Mateo County Victory Garden Supervisor after America's entry into World War II. Jum Morris turned over unused acreage at the Delaware campus for patriotic agriculture. A federally assisted canning program opened on the Baldwin campus in 1943.

and fruit had been processed by September 1944; by the end of the year, the center boasted a total of 108,000 cans. The facility received the top rating of all 57 centers in California. (By 1947, the canning center had been responsible for 374,483 cans of food.)

Still dissatisfied with his success, Klyver made agreements with farmers on San Mateo's Coastside to provide surplus produce. He even worked with fish sources at Princeton to purchase entire truckloads of tuna.

The Community Canning Center became a town focal point with people from every station of life participating. Vivid in the memories of many were efforts of the Sisters of Mercy from Burlingame who, during summer months, participated in canning. The building was hot and full of steam; nevertheless the sisters, in heavy black-woolen habits and stiffly starched cowls, continued their efforts. It must have seemed, said Jim Tormey, that they were "undergoing part of purgatory."

While food was being canned in one of the college's 'temporary' buildings, another 'temporary' building, in 1942, was thrown into use as the San Mateo County Blood Bank. This obvious expedient lasted throughout both World War II and the Korean War. A total of 76,547 pints of blood were donated on the Baldwin campus. (The 'temporary' buildings were destroyed in 1955.)

San Mateo Junior College also became the center of civil defense and civilian education programs for the entire county.

In his 1941-1942 budget, before America entered the war, Jum Morris, believing that the nation's involvement was not far off, added an item for between $35,000 and $40,000. These funds, about which the board was understandably nervous, were to be utilized only in an 'emergency' situation.

Barely had Japanese bombs begun to fall at Pearl Harbor than Morris announced that the college would undertake to finance civilian defense training whether or not additional state funding became available.

Ultimately the college received partial reimbursement. Still, the faculty handled first aid and other essential classes for county residents from Pescadero to San Francisco. Instructor Leonora Brem, employed in 1924 to teach physical education, taught 20 different first aid courses during the war.

"That's when I had boys in class for the first time," recalled Brem.

The financial crisis was in part weathered because demands for other kinds of classes declined and enrollments fell off. Many teachers entered government or military service. There was a total of 72 faculty members (including administrators) in 1940; by 1945 that number had been reduced to 27.

Enrollment plummeted to one quarter of the pre-war norm as male students either enlisted or were drafted. Donna Davis, chair of the Art Department, remembered that "under the pressure of emergency activities and regularly scheduled work, the middle of semesters telescoped and disappeared, leaving only sudden beginnings and swift endings to check the passing of our 'ghost' classes."

Instructor "Sy" Bashor, a lieutenant commander in the U.S. Naval Reserve, was called to active duty in early 1941. He was assigned to a supply center in San Francisco. With uniformity, San Mateo Junior College graduates seeking Navy commissions sought out Bashor for recommendations. Raymond Hemming ('39), who himself rose to the rank of rear admiral in the U.S. Naval Reserve, stated that Bashor was so deluged with requests that secretaries were required to work overtime to keep up. "You could run for president on what Sy wrote about you," stated Hemming. It is estimated that Bashor wrote 500 letters of recommendation.

Varsity sports programs were abandoned between 1943 and 1945. Physical education instructors attempted to keep the spirit of competition alive through a rigid program of individual fitness and intramural sports.

Many campus clubs and organizations, typically male dominated, were taken over by women. In fall 1944, eight of nine on *The San Matean* staff were women; seven of nine working on *The Campus* were women. Of the 22 members in music instructor Frederic Roehr's A Cappella Choir, only two were men.

Construction of the new campus on Delaware, delayed by the war, had begun in 1939. Many assumed that it would be resumed immediately after the peace.

After U.S. entry into World War II, history instructor Sy Bashor, a commander in the Navy, wrote almost 500 letters recommending former students for commissions. One, Raymond Hemming ('39) is pictured at the time of his commissioning in 1942. In addition to establishing the largest accounting firm in Northern California, Hemming rose to the rank of rear admiral in the U.S. Naval Reserve.

However, in the years after 1945, it soon became evident to many educators that there was something very wrong with the college's planning. As a result of the war, in the decade after 1940, the county population expanded by 110 percent. An unexpected post-war baby boom had begun. As early as 1947, kindergarten enrollments were rising noticeably and the number of children attending pre-schools was increasing.

In the county and in the nation, family homes were springing up like mushrooms. Nationwide in 1947, there were 750,000 under construction. This was up 24 percent from 1941, the last great building year before the war.

San Mateo County mirrored the national building spree. School bonds were happily approved by voters. In November 1947, South San Franciscans okayed $1.5 million for a high school and an elementary school. Simultaneously, a bond issue was passed for a high school in the Sequoia High School District to be built in the Menlo Park-Ravenswood area. The following year, workmen began a $675,560 addition to Capuchino High School in San Bruno, and added 10 classrooms and a gymnasium to Redwood City High School.

By the end of 1948, school construction crews were at work in Menlo Park, Atherton, Redwood City, San Mateo, Burlingame, Millbrae, Sharps Park and Pescadero.

Simple projections made it abundantly clear; existing junior college facilities would soon be woefully inadequate. Even if construction on the Delaware campus resumed, it would never adequately serve the needs of the county. Thus, even in 1947, it was apparent that by the 1960s a new campus would be essential.

Barely had the war ended than college officials began eying Coyote Point as a potential site for a new campus—at least as a temporary expedient to accommodate thousands of students expected to materialize.

The site, abandoned in January 1947 by the government, had been the U.S. Merchant Marine Basic Training School since 1942.

UNITED STATES MERCHANT MARINE CADET SCHOOL

The men of the U.S. Merchant Marine were the unsung heroes of World War II. Without fanfare or patriotic send-off, thousands went down to the sea in ships. The fleet was decimated.

Shipyards boomed. More than 282,000 builders were employed in California by 1943. Henry J. Kaiser, one of many contractors, was turning out a new freighter every 10 hours.

Providing officers for these ships became a major problem. That's why, in August 1942, the Merchant Marine Cadet School opened at Coyote Point, or San Mateo Point as the Navy preferred to call it. The school provided accelerated courses for deck and engineering officers. This was the largest of two such centers in the nation.

The 365-acre property, forested by eucalyptus, had been the site of a bathing beach in the 1890s and an amusement park in the early 1920s. Thereafter, it was largely ignored.

Construction of the school began June 25, 1942, blazing paths through eucalyptus and poison oak which had grown wild for almost 70 years. The school, a miracle of wartime construction, included 14 redwood barracks, classrooms, a gymnasium, machine shop and the latest maritime equipment. Essential construction was completed in just 65 days,

although work continued until the end of the year.

Additions included a pool to acquaint cadets with techniques of swimming through debris and oil burning on an ocean surface. A 42-foot mast was erected as an aid to teaching rigging and various aspects of seamanship.

The basic course turned out midshipmen in 90 days. Graduates went to sea for six months, followed by a year of advanced work at the Merchant Marine Academy at Kings Point, New York. The aim was to qualify third mates or third assistant engineering officers in 22 months, equivalent to a four-year course at one of the military academies.

A 30-foot tower was built on a pier extending into deep water. Cadets were required to climb to the top and dive into the bay. This exercise was essential because of the frequency with which mariners were required to leap from sinking ships into turbulent waters. Those who refused to dive were deemed "study casualties" and dropped from the class.

Steamship companies clamored for graduates. By June 1944, there had been 4,111.

In January 1947, budget cuts forced closure of the facility which had become a million dollar a year operation.

San Mateo County had shown interest in acquiring Coyote Point for recreational purposes and had begun buying parcels of the property since the 1920s. This effort was short circuited by wartime emergency. County officials now argued that whereas a college campus at Coyote Point would serve several thousand students annually, more than a million people a year could be expected to use it if placed in the hands of the recreation department. Furthermore, there were no other suitable sites for a park-like development in that region of the county.

Jum Morris was equally strong willed. He believed that vacant academy buildings, at least temporarily, would be ideal for housing classes swollen by large numbers of returning veterans.

County officials finally, albeit reluctantly, agreed to cooperate. The campus could be located at Coyote Point until enrollments leveled off and returned to pre-war numbers. At that time, the County Park and Recreation Department would take over. The college leased 19 acres, acquiring at the same time the right to use Merchant Marine buildings. (There were government strings attached to the deal; the college was required to maintain facilities there for 500 men which could be taken over by the government on short notice in the event of national emergency. This requirement was to remain in effect for 20 years. The Navy continued to use the area on weekends for reserve classes and held a portion of Coyote Point until July 1955.)

Although acquisition of Coyote Point made the college unique among academic institutions in that it now occupied three widely dispersed locations, the press was elated by the compromise. No better example of reconversion of a wartime facility into the uses of peace could be found than "this forging of a sword into a ploughshare."

Classes at the Point opened in September 1947. Until 1955 when Baldwin was finally abandoned (and it became a Navy recruiting facility), classes were taught simultaneously on three campuses. The new property was approximately a mile from Delaware. Jum Morris maintained an office on each campus. A small fleet of rambling buses shuttled students between sites. Efforts were made to keep commuting to a minimum.

Instructor Fanny Baggley taught typing and shorthand. She specialized in helping soldiers who had lost fingers or hands during the war. Each veteran became a special challenge for her and she worked out unique programs so that each could excel in spite of a disability.

Science and mathematics classes along with shop courses were scheduled at Delaware. Art and business classes were reserved for Baldwin. Most other academic courses were taught at Coyote Point. Rules were clear and inflexible. Students were allowed to sign up for consecutive classes at Coyote Point and Delaware or at Baldwin and Delaware. The distance between Baldwin and Coyote Point made it impossible to move between the two campuses in the 10 minutes allotted.

Entry gates to the new campus were marked in gilt letters: "Maritime Commission Academy." Students grumbled. A new sign identifying it as "San Mateo Junior College" wasn't erected until 1952.

The road from the highway into Coyote Point was an experience few who traveled on it ever forgot. It was narrow, winding and riddled with deep crevices and erosion scars. Unpaved parking lots pitted with deep holes became an ongoing joke. Students spoke seriously about the three Cadillacs that "went down last winter and weren't found until June."

Surplus buildings at the Point were a less than perfect expedient. The college gained use of an infirmary and gymnasium with adjoining athletic fields and a swimming pool. Whereas the pool was used by the Physical Education Department, "it scared the instructors spitless." It had been used during the war by cadets practicing drills to abandon ship. Thus, the deep end was 20 feet. Instructors worried that if a student went to the bottom, it would be almost impossible to get him out.

The Commandant's House, former residence of Maritime Academy's commanding officer, a one-story, relatively modern L-shaped structure, was set among a picturesque grove of eucalyptus trees. The dwelling, along with its spacious sheltered patio, was used for meetings of college trustees, faculty and students. Connie Morse remembers it was a great "party house."

The Merchant Marine chapel, perched on the edge of San Francisco Bay, was transformed into the college library. But unquestionably the most popular building on campus was Matson Hall which served as the cafeteria. Students gathered there to eat, study or just plain socialize.

Adding to the popular appeal of Matson Hall was the ever-playing jukebox,

Many veterans, patients at Dibble General Hospital in Menlo Park, attended San Mateo Junior College as part of their therapy. This photograph is of Sgt. James F. De Liste talking with student Jane Davis. De Liste took courses while undergoing surgery to have shrapnel removed from his face.

*Students going to class at Coyote Point.
Though inadequate for academic
pursuits, the Merchant Marine billets
were warmly remembered by those who
attended. Faculty members seemed
preoccupied with campus inadequacies.*

*The Merchant Marine chapel became
the library. When the campus moved in
1963, the new library wasn't yet
finished. Thus, this building continued
to serve. Students at College Heights
made book requests; a book mobile
made four trips per day to Coyote Point.*

a device much appreciated by many and hated by the more serious students who
wanted to use break time to study. Faculty members continually railed against
the blaring music box.

By 1957, cafeteria personnel at Coyote Point were serving 2,000 students
a day. Hot lunches were offered from 11:30 a.m. to 1:30 p.m. Hamburgers
and snacks were available for longer periods. A snack bar opened at 8 a.m. and
closed at 4:30 p.m.

Wood partitions in barn-like barracks created classrooms. English instructor Betty Pex noted that walls at the Point were paper thin. "There was
virtually no privacy." Each department had a single telephone for faculty use.
Students in class could clearly hear lectures being given in adjacent rooms or
an instructor writing on the blackboard from the other side of a wall.

Access to many faculty offices could only be gained by first passing
through a classroom. If there was a lecture in session, an instructor was imprisoned in his office, and students had no access. A few of the classrooms were
especially unusual in shape. They were about 15 feet long and three rows of
chairs deep. "Maintaining eye contact with students was like doing it at a tennis match," remarked Pex.

The old buildings had been rapidly constructed and had not been built to
last. "Coyote Point was always full of surprises," stated Pex. "When I went to
open a window I didn't know whether it would open or fall off the frame onto
the ground."

Coyote Point's physical location on the shore of the bay offered other problems. The campus was directly under the landing pattern to San Francisco
International Airport. "Planes were constantly going overhead, rattling the
buildings," concluded Pex.

Allan Brown, who returned to teach political science at San Mateo following graduation from Stanford, emphasized that teaching conditions were
"nightmarish." Rumbling airplane noise constantly interrupted lectures.
Especially frustrated, one day Brown decided to mark the blackboard each
time his lecture was interrupted by a plane. At the end of 30 minutes, there
were 19 marks on the board.

Faculty and students alike complained about the ineffectiveness and noise of the steam heating system. Many instructors simply turned it off to end the noise.

The heating plant consisted of a boiler taken from an old U.S. Naval vessel, probably a destroyer, recalled Philip C. Garlington who came to San Mateo in 1956 as Dean of Instruction. Eroding steam pipes leading to the buildings were only a few inches underground. Although the pipes were in terrible condition, when the district began developing the campus, a decision was reached not to invest money in maintenance "unnecessarily."

During the college's last years at the Point, many of the pipes burst. Each time one let go it sent up a spout of hot steam. Garlington added that they were patched in a sort of "band-aid" manner, but the campus often "resembled a Yellowstone Park geyser basin, and we all watched carefully where we walked."

Students took perverse delight in these conditions, referring to the geysers of steam as "Mauna Loa." A writer in *The San Matean* noted that "frantic efforts" were being made to repair the persistent volcano which some "enraged students had trained to swallow up teachers." The writer noted that "the instructor of Sanskrit has been reported missing."

Two of the former billets, out near the harbor, were retained for use as dormitories to house single male students on a first come, first served basis. These offered the most Spartan of living conditions. The buildings received paint and a necessary facelift from the Mothers Club under the experienced gaze of Carlena Morris. No food service was provided in the dormitories. Residents were expected to eat at the nearby cafeteria building.

The dorms were an ongoing source of difficulty. Philip Morse, assistant to the dean of students, remembered that there were always wild parties and that significant drinking went on. "Then they'd try to tear the place up. But only twice did things really get out of control and did police have to be called."

In June 1948, football coach McFadden wrote Jum Morris bemoaning that greater supervision was required in the Coyote Point Men's Dormitory to bring about control of resident students. He complained of rowdies and so much noise that "many students wanting to study won't live here."

Buildings at Coyote Point had been rapidly constructed and were full of surprises. "When I went to open a window, I didn't know whether it would open or fall out of the frame onto the ground," reported instructor Betty Pex.

Efforts were also made to accommodate married students immediately after the war by opening housing at Campus Manor on the Delaware campus. These structures, built in 1946 with prefabricated and temporary material, consisted of two dormitories and four apartment units. Operated by the San Mateo County Housing Authority, Campus Manor didn't come under control of the college district until 1953. College and county officials at that time inspected the units and found them far below health standards. Although the buildings had served the college well for eight years, they were demolished in July 1954.

Post-war enrollment skyrocketed. Seats were filled by returning veterans who were collecting payments under the G.I. Bill of Rights. The student body numbered 1,800 in 1946. In September 1947, 2,200 had registered and that number was expected to increase by 200 at the end of the first week. Thirty-five graduated in 1945; 307 received diplomas in 1949.

Post-war students seemed more serious. Former veterans were found to have well defined goals. Instructor Dorothy Herrington stated that they had objectives and a purpose for going to college. "They were more serious mind-ed...that was very interesting and...gratifying."

Although Coyote Point was never an ideal college campus and students enjoyed complaining about everything from parking to cafeteria food, the move there brought about, after more than a decade of war and Depression, a reawakening of that intangible substance known as college spirit.

During the first years at Coyote Point, the campus was still marked with the sign: Maritime Commission Academy. After more than five years, a College of San Mateo sign was erected.

Students had exhibited pride in their college from the beginning. In November 1931, on the eve of San Mateo Junior College's tenth anniversary, Earle Marsh ('32) suggested celebrating the event with a reunion or Alumni Day.

The first such event was scheduled at the Baldwin campus, April 3, 1932. By then, its promoters were referring to it as Homecoming. The campus swarmed with "old grads." The morning started with a mammoth rally conducted by the cheer leading squad. A telegram was read from John Roberts ('23), the *first* and *only* student to graduate from San Mateo Junior College that year (he was a transfer student from the University of Washington). At noon there was a luncheon on the front lawn and throughout the day the halls teemed with returning graduates visiting former instructors. Later in the afternoon, the Associated Women Students (A.W.S.) hosted an alumni tea.

Thereafter and until the eve of World War II when such "frivolous activities" were suspended, Homecoming became an annual event. (Plans for the bonfire were scrapped in 1933 despite vigorous collection of wood and other burnable materials. Student leaders voted that, because of the economic crisis in the nation, the wood should be given to needy people for heating.)

Homecoming was reintroduced at Coyote Point in the fall of 1949. The event was characterized by a return of the traditional bonfire (constructed by the Engineers Club) on the beach, a queen contest, parade, football game and finally a dance in the college gymnasium. These noisy events grew bigger and more spectacular every year. Thousands participated.

Throughout the 1950s, music instructor Bud Young's blue and white sharply uniformed San Mateo Junior College Bulldog Marching Band, led a mammoth parade through the streets of San Mateo and Burlingame.

Throughout the 1950s under the direction of music instructor Bud Young, the Bulldog Marching Band, dressed in blue and white, led parades through the streets of San Mateo and Burlingame. Football games weren't complete without the band's half-time presentation.

Homecoming 1955, characterized as "Fantasy Royale," featured 12 floats. That year some of the edge was taken off the excitement when pesky arsonists from San Francisco City College took advantage of an absence of guards and prematurely set the half-constructed bonfire ablaze. Engineering students quickly recouped and constructed another in time for the scheduled gala event.

The next year, San Mateo police estimated 3,000 students, alumni and guests participated in the gala. The International Relations Club walked away with the first place award, $10 for the most outstanding float.

Another float that year carried the Homecoming queen. Competition for queen was fierce, a much sought after honor bestowed upon "the loveliest coed on the campus." The Queen's Float was decorated with 50,000 student-made Kleenex flowers. A Coronation Ball was held in the Men's Gymnasium where the newly crowned queen was presented with an elegant trophy made by Granite Brothers.

Climaxing the exciting Homecoming activities was a gala ball, either in Matson Hall or the Men's Gymnasium on Second Avenue. Music was provided by music instructor Dick Crest (Richard Louis Cresta), himself a college alumnus ('49), and his 12-piece student dance orchestra.

Women students at the Point delighted in staging annual slumber parties in the gymnasium. Highlighting these springtime events were barbecues with hot dogs, potato salad, cocoa, milk and coffee.

"Girls," a word still commonly used in the 1950s, played badminton, basketball and ping pong. Typically they roughhoused with pillow and mattress fights, then sang camp songs. When the weather was warm, a midnight swim in the pool was added to the busy schedule. The jukebox blared and strange forms bopped far into the night. At last, all bedded down in sleeping bags on the gym floor. Orange juice, milk and hot donuts were served for breakfast.

Guys had parties of their own. With their dads and male faculty members, boys participated in semi-annual *smokers* at Matson Hall. Entry for the evening cost 35 cents.

Smokers usually featured live entertainment, movies and door prizes. Ice cream and cigarettes were free. The only women admitted were the finalists in

During the post-World War II decade, the sexual balance along the peninsula re-established itself. Many new relationships were made in the Coyote Point gymnasium where college dances were scheduled.

the Homecoming queen contest who paraded before the all-male audience "to be scrutinized and appreciated."

Women students in March 1958, staged a "Gals' Puffer," the first in the history of the college. Refreshments were served "along with free cigarettes for those who smoke." They were reminded, however, that they need not be among the puffers to have a good time. "Free candy cigarettes will also be given."

J um Morris, president and superintendent of the San Mateo Junior College District, was attending a basketball game and dance in the college gymnasium on Second Avenue Feb. 22, 1952. There he suffered the heart attack which, two days later, proved fatal. He was 64 years old.

Vocational courses have been a major part of the college curriculum since the 1930s. Here are students involved in aeronautics at the Delaware campus after World War II.

He had been at the helm of the college for 21 years. Few administrators have been better known. During later years, many students knew him simply as "Jum." His office door was always open and he was remembered best at Baldwin where students counted on him to meet them at "Nicotine Bridge" for a cigarette. He was always approachable. Those with complaints about what was going on told Morris directly.

When Morris had come to San Mateo in 1931, a college education was reserved almost exclusively for would-be white collar workers. Morris spearheaded the movement that changed all that. Under his leadership vocational training was introduced to prepare students for trade apprenticeship requirements and other occupations requiring specified subject matter and training in a skill.

By the mid-1950s, these programs included aeronautics, agriculture, architectural drafting, bookkeeping and accounting, various building trades, ceramics, commercial art, cosmetology, dental assisting, vocational nursing, electronics and radio, secretarial training and apprentice training in different trades.

Though Morris died in February, some faculty looked upon an article which appeared in the *San Francisco Chronicle*, June 15, 1952, as one of

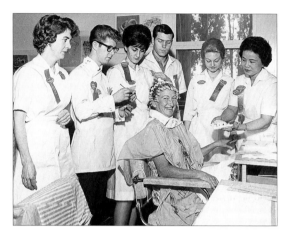

Since the 1950s, San Mateo has been renowned for cosmetology. Students competed regularly in the International Hairstyling Olympics, often in Europe. While usually satisfied, there had been complaints. During the 1970s, one unhappy woman, still wearing her plastic smock, hiked the length of the campus and stormed into the president's office. "What are you going to do about this," she demanded pointing at her hair. David Mertes, usually the ultimate gentleman and diplomat, shook his head and laughed, "Sorry, I don't do hair."

Morris' most memorable epitaphs. The headline read: "Graduate as a Plumber and Get a College Degree."

San Mateo Junior College's thirtieth commencement, staged in Hillsborough's Woodland Amphitheater, saw 295 students pick up Associate of Arts degrees. Of this number, all clad in academic caps and gowns, 52 were plumbers.

"Along with being a specialist in the application of the plumber's friend and the pipe wrench, he is something of an expert on American institutions, state government, hygiene and the English language." On-the-job training certified these individuals as master craftsmen and classroom instruction qualified them as an Associate of Arts. As far as Morris had been concerned, such education added strength to American democracy.

Not long after Morris' death, San Mateo students began a movement to change the name of the college. Many of California's junior colleges had already dropped the word "junior" from their titles. Some students found the word demeaning if not an outright misrepresentation. It implied that the role of the junior college was simply to provide the first two years of a four-year education.

By April of 1953, many San Mateo faculty members agreed with students that dropping the "junior" would noticeably raise the stature of the college. Student body officers conducted a poll participated in by 329 students. Seventy-two percent favored a name change. Names suggested were San Mateo College, San Mateo City College and Peninsula College. The name College of San Mateo was suggested by 62 participating in the survey.

Marlin Gill wrote in *The San Matean* (April 16, 1953) that the name College of San Mateo "would be a standing memorial to the junior college's past president, Charles S. Morris. The initials of the new name (CSM) would be the same as those of President Morris' initials. The school radio station already bears the code name KCSM."

County Superintendent of Schools James Tormey, interviewed during the 1970s, emphatically stated that the initials CSM were chosen as a memorial to Morris. The board of trustees evaluated the request and concurred with the wishes of the students. San Mateo Junior College became College of San Mateo, a year later, on April 14, 1954.

"He looks like he was weaned on a pickle," a number of instructors said of Elon Hildreth when the new president was named in April 1952. Hildreth was a graduate of the University of California, a former junior high school principal and junior college administrator in Southern California. A lackluster personality, Hildreth was totally ill-equipped to fill the giant shoes left by Jum Morris.

While some considered Hildreth a fairly competent administrator and "fine fellow," he never attempted to establish a cordial working relationship with the community. Worse, through his condescending nature, he alienated the American Association of University Women and the League of Women Voters who attacked him for his lack of planning ability. He refused to share college accreditation reports with leaders of the womens' groups who requested them. Hildreth explained that his refusal was based on the fact that the documents contained a great deal of educational jargon and commented that "*women* wouldn't be able to understand them."

"He was not a man for his times," stated Eleanore D. Nettle who became a candidate for the college's board of trustees in opposition to Hildreth. Equally damaging, during his brief tenure, he clearly established himself as an enemy of the county's two most powerful newspaper editors, J. Hart Clinton of the *San Mateo Times* and James Woods of the *Burlingame Advance Star*. Both attacked him relentlessly.

They believed that Hildreth had broken a "gentlemen's agreement" with the county. That is, the understanding that after the post-war boom, the college would turn Coyote Point over to the county for use as a public recreational area.

Hildreth was totally enamored with Coyote Point as the site for a new college. He declared that the site was almost ideally situated for easy access and

Elon Hildreth replaced Jum Morris in 1952. It would have taken a giant to fill Morris' shoes. Hildreth lacked stature, and his tenure at San Mateo was brief. After less than four years, he accepted an educational position in Southeast Asia.

Eleanore D. Nettle, a student at San Mateo during the 1930s, declared that Elon Hildreth "was not a man for his times." She ran for the board of trustees and was elected in 1956. She served 33 years, attending almost 800 board meetings and acting nine times as president. She was instrumental in the building of College Heights and the expansion of the college district, shepherding establishment of Cañada College (Redwood City) in 1968 and Skyline College (San Bruno) in 1969.

student convenience. To critics who argued that the new campus should be put in the hills, he responded that such would require quarrying and grading and send construction costs skyrocketing.

The tranquil setting of Coyote Point, among eucalyptus groves on the edge of the bay, fit his concept of where a college should be placed. Hildreth pooh-poohed naysayers who predicted that airport noise would only become worse. The noise question, he declared, was grossly exaggerated. "What makes the planes seem so noisy is that the campus is so unusually quiet. Aircraft noises would be far worse reverberating in the hills." Opponents simmered when he invited distinguished Southern California architect Richard Neutra to draw plans for a campus among the trees.

As if to solidify his hold on Coyote Point property, in December 1952, Hildreth announced that he and his wife intended to make the Commandant's House their home. Thus, to the dissatisfaction of both community leaders and instructors, he ended the tradition of its use for meetings by students, faculty and trustees.

In making the move, Hildreth explained that the "President's Home" would put him in closer proximity to students and be a rallying point for everyone in support of Coyote Point college. He planned faculty lunches, fashion shows, faculty wives and alumni meetings, holiday teas and faculty receptions.

Writing to trustees in the summer of 1954, Hildreth noted that, during the previous school year, he and his wife had used the President's Home as the site of 47 different public or semi-public functions with 1,276 people having been entertained during the first semester and 1,413 in the second.

Hildreth unsuccessfully attempted to mollify his opposition, offering to develop athletic facilities at Coyote Point jointly with the county. But officials weren't about to be assuaged. Recreation commissioners looked upon the presence of the college at Coyote Point as a threat to the entire county park system. Hildreth's stance, recreation people felt, constituted premeditated deception.

The final straw, however, came in 1954 after Hildreth returned from a trip to Washington, D.C., where his major effort had been to assure college control of Coyote Point. Without approval from the board of trustees, he signed documents relinquishing control of the Baldwin campus to the Navy for a few dollars a year. In return the college retained its still tenuous lease on Coyote Point.

Board members were flabbergasted. Trustees had always given college administrators considerable leeway. But the determined Hildreth had usurped their prerogatives. The president's contract was not renewed.

In an affront that left Hildreth mortally wounded, in March 1955, the board dropped Coyote Point from any future consideration as a possible one-site campus of the college.

Just before Christmas 1955, Hildreth resigned because of "ill health." A few months later, it was learned in San Mateo that the former president had accepted a position with the U.S. State Department. He was sent to Saigon, Vietnam, to assist in reorganization of the South Vietnamese schools and, in the process, to help assure the "continuing health of that nation's democratic tradition."

The photograph of Julio Bortolazzo, attached to his employment application in 1956, gave no hint of the dynamic personality he possessed or charismatic leadership he would provide.

College of San Mateo had become the community stalking-horse. Local newspapers blasted that at its present rate of progress, the college might get a new campus somewhere around the year 2000. Maybe.

Faculty morale sagged. Accreditation was in doubt. The major campus was entering advanced stages of deterioration. There were no long-range educational plans. And, had students been queried, they most certainly would have complained that parking was woefully inadequate.

The place was in a foundering state of uncertainty. Community leaders, once so supportive of the junior college, wondered aloud if the experiment had failed and if San Mateo needed such an institution at all.

Exasperated trustees carefully studied a field of 33 applicants for president before finally offering the position to 40-year old Julio Bortolazzo, then president of Stockton Junior College since 1952.

"I have carefully reviewed your list of qualifications for the position and sincerely hope that I meet most of your requirements," Bortolazzo had humbly written in his letter of application dated Feb. 20, 1956.

Philip C. Garlington, an administrator at Stockton College, was invited by Bortolazzo to be dean of instruction at San Mateo. Garlington was later the founding president of Skyline College (San Bruno).

He enclosed a small snapshot of himself, seated on the edge of a neat desk, wearing a light-colored nondescript suit, white shirt and clip-on bow tie. His ordinary appearance perhaps helped camouflage the fact that Bortolazzo was one of the most dynamic educational reformers of his day.

Bortolazzo came aboard July 1, 1956. Within hours of his taking over, the College of San Mateo lurched ahead and has never looked back.

The new president was an educational trouble-shooter. Philip C. Garlington, a dean at Stockton College who was coaxed by Bortolazzo to become College of San Mateo's Dean of Instruction in 1958, noted that his boss "seemed to prefer tough challenges to smooth sailing...he thrived on getting a major crisis or a big problem to overcome." Garlington stated emphatically that Bortolazzo became "one of the most outstanding educational leaders in the history of California's community colleges."

Years later a reporter wrote that the dynamic, effervescent Bortolazzo was "an aggressive educator with a volatile Latin temperament" who conquered his problems with "a zest that rocketed his school from the doldrums to a proud position among the front ranks of California junior colleges."

College trustee Eleanore D. Nettle, elected in 1956, perhaps worded it most succinctly when she stated that Bortolazzo was a "bulldozer with brains."

Born in Santa Barbara (1915), Julio Lorenzo Bortolazzo was the son of an Italian immigrant peasant farmer, and later grocer, who had come to America in 1910. The boy's name was really "Giulio," but when he started school in Santa Barbara, teachers spelled it the Spanish way. The Italian-speaking lad was unable to correct them at the time and, later in life, never corrected the spelling.

Bortolazzo not only possessed the charismatic personality necessary to accomplish his goals, he had more than the requisite education. He'd graduated with a bachelor's degree in history and education from Santa Barbara State College (1936). Later, he earned a master's of science from the University of Southern California (1939) and both a master's (1942) and doctorate (1949) in education from Harvard University.

The man was a near magician at winning popular support for education. Serving as superintendent of schools in Lake Oswego, Oregon (1950-1952), he established and supervised construction of a new high school. As president of Stockton College, he'd been responsible for building an entirely new campus. During his career he tackled 18 tax and bond elections, winning 17. In San Mateo County, he not only planned and guided the building of College of San Mateo but Cañada and Skyline colleges as well. Overall, it is conservatively estimated that his efforts were responsible for almost $100 million in educational construction.

Bortolazzo's goal in San Mateo was a new campus, but not one located at Coyote Point. Often described as an impatient sort, the college president admitted to a reporter: "Everybody knows I want things done yesterday." He put pressure on his subordinates to achieve, but all readily admitted that he drove himself harder.

To generate community support, without which he had no hope of success, 30 days after arriving on campus, he formed a "blue ribbon" advisory committee of distinguished citizens to evaluate the present status of the district and recommend a course of action to meet the growing needs of the college. Selected as co-chairmen were J. Hart Clinton, editor and publisher of the *San Mateo Times* and James Woods, publisher of the *Burlingame Advance Star.* "Choosing Clinton and Woods as the co-chairs of the committee was a master stroke," stated Bortolazzo's assistant William Goss.

A meeting of three Harvard men in 1960. J. Hart Clinton (left), Bortolazzo and Harvard President James Conant. Clinton, publisher-editor of the San Mateo Times, *co-chaired Bortolazzo's Blue Ribbon Committee which recommended the move to College Heights.*

The 27-member Citizens Committee held its first meeting in November 1956. The following January, it recommended immediate action to acquire a site in the San Mateo area. Following more than 30 meetings and innumerable site inspections, it presented the board of trustees with a final report. Committee members concluded that San Mateo County not only needed a community college, it would ultimately require more than one. The first should be built in the hills west of town overlooking San Mateo.

Determined to excite the community about the projected college, during his first year, Bortolazzo embarked on a speaking marathon. "He was absolutely brilliant when it came to the handling of community affairs," remarked Goss. Bortolazzo's personal schedule was backbreaking. Often accompanied

William Goss was one of the few people known by Bortolazzo when the latter arrived in San Mateo. He served as an administrative assistant and later vice president. Goss was also the founding president of Cañada College (Redwood City).

by Goss, who was responsible for slides, charts and backup materials, Bortolazzo faced hundreds of organizations, many of them initially hostile, speaking to as many as three groups a day. "He was admired for his vigor and enthusiasm," added Goss.

The president planned his calendar to meet a different organization every night of the week. Goss recalled one occasion when he did not get home from an evening meeting until 12:45 a.m. He checked his calendar and found that Bortolazzo had scheduled the next session for 7 a.m.

Realtors opposed plans for a college. Bortolazzo waded into the heart of the enemy camp to spar with real estate agents. He argued that quality public education sells homes. In a matter of hours, they joined the new college bandwagon.

So effectively was the college's message delivered that, Oct. 15, 1957, residents of the county, by a margin of three to one, approved a $5.9 million bond issue for the new College Heights campus.

"This day will live in community history…and I predict that College of San Mateo will come to stand for a new summit in junior college performance and achievement," Bortolazzo told 100 educators and civic leaders who braved

Groundbreaking for College Heights was a pleasant task undertaken by trustees in October 1960. Trustee U.S. Simonds, assisted by Trustee Eleanore D. Nettle, turned the first dirt.

heavy winds to attend the groundbreaking ceremony Oct. 21, 1960. The first shovelful of earth was turned at 11:30 a.m. U.S. Simonds, Chairman of the Board of Trustees, was first to make the dirt fly.

The land, 153 acres high on a quiet green hill looking eastward over the rooftops of San Mateo, had been ranch property of building contractor L.C. Smith. Architectural critic Allan Temko described the site as one of "natural splendor of the kind fast vanishing in urban California." The acreage was "scored by deep ravines, dotted with oaks and eucalyptus and commanding a magnificent view of the bay."

The college district acquired this property at a cost of $7,280 per acre following a successful eminent domain suit. Years later, Bortolazzo commented that acquisition of the land had been "the best buy since Manhattan was acquired from the Indians."

Participants in the groundbreaking who wandered across the vast acreage, saw vestiges of L.C. Smith's demolished horse barns (near where the tennis courts were ultimately built) and fields in which polo ponies grazed and gaited horses had trained on a small oval track, all poignant reminders of the San Mateo of a previous generation.

John Carl Warnecke was a graduate of Stanford with advanced study in architecture at Harvard. He was commonly referred to by the press as "one of America's leading architects."

Warnecke began drawing plans for College Heights in summer, 1957. It is obvious, from correspondence found in the presidential archives, that his inspiration was Frank Lloyd Wright's dramatic and futuristic Florida Southern College, planned in 1936. The files contained photos of the Lakeland, Florida institution from *Architectural Forum* (September 1952) and Warnecke's correspondence to acquire the plans. Warnecke's efforts were accelerated after successful passage of the bond issue.

Forty-three and scion of a second generation West Coast architectural family, Warnecke was recognized internationally for his work. To his credit

College Heights, as the 153-acre site appeared on the eve of development. As much as 30 feet of soil was carved away to create the building area.

Architect John Carl Warnecke, principal designer of College Heights, came with an international reputation.

A virtual motor pool of heavy equipment was required to cut through underbrush and carve away layers of clay.

were designs for the United States Embassy in Bangkok, the state capitol of Hawaii, the American International Insurance building in Tokyo and most recently, his restoration of the Lafayette Square section of Washington, D.C. He designed eight buildings for the University of California.

Site preparation for College of San Mateo began in February 1960. Original contours were changed by grading to provide plateau areas for principal buildings. Thirty feet of soil was cut away from the primary building site. Series of terraces were carved into the easterly side of the property to be used for physical education and community recreation fields and courts.

More than a million and a quarter cubic yards of earth were moved as part of a balanced cut-and-fill program. Grading, accomplished by the Wunderlich Co., was completed by October.

Bortolazzo promised that this would be a "no frills campus without sacrificing sophistication." The firm of Theo G. Meyer and Sons received the contract for construction of 10 buildings.

Construction, characterized by almost constant bickering between college officials and contractors and the levying of ominous penalty fees against contractors, was agonizingly slow. It had been hoped that classes at College Heights would open in September 1962; the project lagged a year behind schedule.

Some delay was caused by unexpected sub-soil conditions and, Bortolazzo admitted, the soil on the site turned out to be "irregular." Where builders expected to encounter rock, they found clay. Before construction could proceed, more than $100,000 had to be spent excavating for deeper caissons and footings for the buildings.

Contractors placed blame for the interminable delays squarely on the shoulders of Bortolazzo and the college board of trustees. They claimed Bortolazzo couldn't make up his mind, which resulted in multiple change orders. In 1965, two years after the campus opened, Meyer brought a $1.8 million suit against College of San Mateo, alleging that completion of the campus was delayed because educators "obstructed and hindered the performance of the contractor."

Not so, the fiery Bortolazzo insisted. He charged that Meyer and Sons had failed to properly schedule and coordinate the work and had skimped on manpower. Work sheets, he said, indicated that there were never more than 325 men on the job at any one time.

"Baloney," countered Meyer. "We've had up to 600 men on the project at one time…the manpower has been sufficient. The soil conditions set the job back some, but what really killed us has been this amazing series of change orders."

Meyer, charging that the college was "penny wise and pound foolish," was especially critical of the role played by Bortolazzo. "He's up here yelling about things…he says he's going to handle the situation himself. Then he admits he can't even use a screwdriver or a hammer."

Following completion of the campus, Bortolazzo looked back with pride on the project, noting that "not a single dollar" had been expended on consultants. "The outstanding professional staff under the able leadership of Bill Goss did it all."

But construction workers found their jobs "intolerable." Turnover was tremendous. "These people claim they want the best, but they don't know what the best is." According to Meyer, many professionals became so disgusted at being told what to do by a bunch of amateurs, they simply quit and went where working conditions were better.

Weldon L. Richards, vice president of the Pacific Co. Engineers and Builders of Berkeley, one of the two major contractors on the site, found working for the college a cause of ongoing frustration. In part he complained about the "unorthodox relationship" between the college and the architectural firm of John Carl Warnecke. "We would get district approval and the architect would rescind it. When the architect approved, the district would rescind it." It was almost impossible. "I asked who was boss and was told to get approval from both."

Arguments notwithstanding, the new College of San Mateo rose like a colossus on the hill. "You see work force after work force. It's not one project but a dozen," wrote *San Mateo Times* reporter George Golding.

With the library's outline completed in the distance, work began on the patio area in front of the Administration Building.

The construction site was an arena of frenzied activity. Roads in all directions were ankle-deep in powdery dust and cluttered with boards, sticks, pipes, hoses and concrete droppings. Architectural style was not extreme. Buildings were "gracefully clean in their simplicity." They appeared massive yet graceful with acres of windows which looked out between narrow pillars. Initially, 27 buildings were constructed of concrete and steel at an average cost of $16 a foot.

Architectural critics cackled with obvious admiration. Bortolazzo and Warnecke strove to create a uniquely collegiate environment as opposed to including design features often associated with secondary schools. The end result conveyed a dignity, distinguishing College Heights as unique. Many felt that it was among the first two-year colleges in the nation "to express the dignity of a university."

The largest class in College of San Mateo history, to that time, graduated from the San Mateo High School Auditorium, June 17, 1962. A total of 439 received diplomas and listened to young San Francisco State economics Professor Thomas Lantos speak on "Closed Minds in a Closed Society."

At 4:30 p.m., Sept. 6, 1963, an "end of an era" ceremony was held at Coyote Point. A Marine color guard lowered the flag in the farewell ritual.

The Delaware campus was sold Feb. 21, 1963, in what was believed to be the biggest sale of public property ever made in the county. For the 30 acres, College of San Mateo received $2,251,600.

"At last, CSM is through with hand-me-downs." Classes at College Heights, scheduled to open Sept. 16, 1963, were once more delayed, until Sept. 30. Bortolazzo declared that shorter holidays would make up for the lost days. (Construction was still far from finished. The sounds of hammers, saws and drills disturbed the academic atmosphere of the campus throughout the rest of 1963 and the next year. Bortolazzo would beg students to be patient with the noise, dust and smell of construction.)

A colossal traffic jam had cars backed up along the just completed Nineteenth Avenue Freeway all the way east to Bayshore Highway. A total of 3,200 automobiles brought 5,621 students to class that day. Although

Bortolazzo and Warnecke strove to create a college rather than secondary school environment. Critics felt that CSM was one of the first community colleges in the nation "to express the dignity of a university."

The weeks after the opening of College Heights were characterized by continual traffic jams as the community sought to adjust to the invasion of automobiles.

extra traffic squads were brought into action, traffic slowed to a walk for long periods between 7 a.m. and 8 a.m. For weeks, automobile commuters, normally accustomed to easy travel, were jolted by unusually long delays around San Mateo.

Parking was nightmarish. Lots west of the campus, near Parrott Drive, had not yet been developed. "It was really wild," stated Bill Goss, "students just parked any place they could." Goss and Business Manager Matt Fasanaro took off their jackets, rolled up sleeves and spent the morning moving rocks and even boulders out of the fields to make room for cars. "No matter how much we planned, we still weren't ready," concluded Goss. Crisis developed when 1,150 more cars arrived on campus than had been expected. After a week of classes, there were still 650 cars parked on overflow, unpaved lots.

Official dedication of College Heights was Dec. 8, 1963. After 41 years of moving from one temporary facility to another, the college was now unified on a single campus. The ceremony began at 2:30 p.m. with a colorful cap and gown procession by the faculty which had swollen in size to 222, fifty-one of whom were newly hired. Instructor Dick Crest conducted the Bulldog Band. A beaming Bortolazzo was disappointed that only 1,200 county residents attended the unveiling. Architect John Carl Warnecke, a special guest, flew in from Washington, D.C., where he had been consulting on the design of a tomb for recently assassinated President John Fitzgerald Kennedy.

At Coyote Point, the college had been restricted to 170,000 square feet, including classroom space at the campus on Delaware. The new campus boasted an expansive 471,000 square feet. There was a Little Theater, an outdoor theater, a planetarium, horticultural center and an educational television station.

"The only thing 'junior' about the new San Mateo Junior College campus is that instruction will still be limited to a two-year curriculum," wrote journalist George Golding.

Architecturally and educationally, although it had not been completed by the opening day of the semester, the dominant building on the new campus was the 49,402-square foot library. It finally opened for student use Nov. 15, 1963.

Before landscaping, buildings appeared stark and monolithic. More than 5,000 students attended the first day of fall 1963.

COLLEGE OF THE AIR

Hundreds of students missed class Sept. 24, 1964, to witness the raising of the television tower, one of the final steps before broadcasting began on KCSM-TV, Channel 14.

The 90-foot tower was set in concrete near the College Heights library. A 53-foot antenna was placed atop the tower. This 143-foot structure weighed nine tons.

KCSM-TV was the second television station in the nation run by a community college. KCSM's ultra high frequency signal could be received as far away as San Jose, Richmond, areas of Oakland and all parts of San Francisco.

The initial broadcast was Oct.13, 1964. Authorization for operation from the Federal Communications Commission arrived only eight minutes before the first broadcast, an hour-long program on health education.

Bob Foster, television critic for the *San Mateo Times* noted that the picture was "pretty fuzzy" because, back then, most people didn't have UHF antennas on home sets. But he added: "The sound was excellent."

Initially, KCSM-TV broadcasted 21 half-hour programs on a six hour per day schedule. The test pattern began at 7:30 a.m.

Since its establishment during the 1920s, the college had been on the cutting edge of broadcast technology. San Mateo Junior College had one of the oldest amateur radio stations in the country, dating from 1925.

Electronics instructor Jake Wiens joined the college faculty in 1939. During World War II, he participated in the Manhattan Project—the development of the atomic bomb. Wiens resumed his position in January 1946.

"I began to experiment with equipment that led to the development of the Frequency Modulation Broadcasting Station at College of San Mateo," stated Wiens. No one so thoroughly deserves the title "father" of an institution. Wiens personally engineered and constructed the broadcasting equipment.

Located at the Baldwin campus, the station went on the air Feb. 13, 1953. KCSM-FM was to stimulate community interest in college activities. Selected classes were taped for radio relay in the evening.

President Bortolazzo made broadcasting a goal at College Heights. A portion of the library's ground floor was set aside for these facilities.

Approximately 100 rooms were wired for closed circuit television.

But faculty and students rebelled against the technology. Instructors saw it as a threat to their job security. Students found the medium frustrating. Bortolazzo admitted that the failure to effectively use television as an educational tool was a disappointment. Successful open circuit broadcasting in 1964 marked the culmination of five years of planning and preparation by Wiens.

The library's location, at the intersection of the two circulating malls, was chosen to make it the college's chief attraction. The striking structure, with a 176-foot front, was finished in gray glass and pierced-masonry screens on three sides, shielding the building from excessive sunlight and glare.

Librarian John Dooley effervesced that the library had been "dark and crowded" at Coyote Point. At College Heights, "it is light and spacious."

From the beginning, the library was organized around the concept of an "instructional materials center." It contained every imaginable adjunct for the teaching process. Not only was there stack space on the mezzanine for 65,000 volumes but complete audio-visual services, recording and preview rooms, an FM radio station and a television studio. The reading room provided space for 250 students with additional seating amid the stacks. Overall, there was four times the amount of space than had been available at Coyote Point.

Librarians boasted that their audio facility, the largest in the state, gave students an opportunity to learn many subjects through listening as well as through the normal facilities for reading. Bortolazzo insisted that CSM's was the most modern and complete audio facility in California and would surely become the focal point of attention from educators all over the country.

Touring the campus one found a series of buildings, the majority of which were two stories, all of reinforced concrete, connected by arcades. They were placed along the two circulation malls. The scale of both the buildings and the malls was never allowed to become small or intimate, a style commonly found in California school construction. Gray heat-absorbing glass was used wherever control of the sun presented a problem.

Faculty, conditioned by Coyote Point's bucolic atmosphere, felt the new college lacked personality. The place seemed to have been designed solely with exteriors in mind. English instructor Jean Wirth complained that each faculty office building was constructed with a single toilet for women's use.

Forty of the college's 153 acres were devoted to physical education. The new 55,813-square foot gymnasium was touted as the finest on the Peninsula. Seating capacity for basketball games was 1,500; auditorium seating capacity was 2,300. Spotlights and auditorium lights supplemented traditional gym lighting which

The College Heights library, known for its unique architecture, became the heart of the institution. During 1995-1996 it was closed for retrofitting, renovation and to make the building more friendly for physically disabled students.

The library, in 1963, contained 65,000 volumes in addition to the most up-to-date audio-visual facilities in the state.

Forty acres at College Heights were set aside for athletics and physical education. The gymnasium seated 1,500 for basketball games and 2,300 for concerts and other events.

was primarily suitable for sports events. While the gymnasium was originally meant to double for rallies and musical events, Galen Marshall, conductor of the Masterworks Chorale, would later comment on the gym's abominable acoustics and its total inadequacy for anything except athletic meets.

Athletic fields east of the gymnasium, constructed on a series of terraces comprising the so-called 'Back Forty' on the southeastern portion of the campus, were carefully created with the hilltop's ever-present winds in mind. They were set below breeze-blocking banks. The baseball field, not completed until 1965, was 65 feet beneath the level of campus buildings.

Although not completed until 1964, a football stadium surrounded by a nine-lane, all-weather track was provided with 4,300 bleacher seats. Dedication of the new field Oct. 17, 1964 was cause for celebration. It was the first home gridiron in the college's 42-year history. (The field received a "baptism of fire" in a Golden Gate Conference clash between College of San Mateo and Diablo Valley College, a matchup the Bulldogs won by an impressive 29 to 13 score. The first touchdown was scored by CSM quarterback Chuck Hunt, No. 19, on an eight yard run around his right end.)

There were ten tennis courts, said by leading club players to be among the finest in Northern California, two swimming pools, eight outdoor basketball courts, six handball and six volleyball courts. The two pools, one designed for water polo and diving, were sheltered west of the gymnasium. Inside the gym, there were 2,700 lockers for men and 2,000 for women.

Landscapers, presented with a challenging situation because of heavy winter rains and frequent high winds on the hilltop, transformed College Heights into a thing of beauty with sweeping stretches of green lawn and carefully selected shrubbery. Otherwise undeveloped hillsides were planted with banks of blooming mesembryanthmum spectablis—ice plant—which prospered almost without care and, in spring, created striking fields of purple.

At the suggestion of Business Manager Matt Fasanaro, grounds were punctuated with hundreds of olive trees, transplanted from an ancient olive orchard owned by the college in Redwood City. (Later in the decade, this property became Cañada College.)

CSM's championship women's volleyball team, 1973. In the two decades that followed, women's athletics were essentially the story of Tom Martinez who coached basketball and softball. He led teams to 1,092 victories, thus according him the honor as having been the "winningest coach in California." He was named conference Coach of the Year 17 different times. Martinez also served five years as head football coach.

Architects regarded the landscaping as an important element of the collegiate atmosphere where good lawns could play a vital role in deciding a student's future by bolstering dreams, rehabilitating spirits or by providing a soft bed for a between-classes nap.

By Bortolazzo's instructions, there were no "keep off the grass" signs. Within a year, however, because of major damage to the lawns caused by masses of students seeking shorter routes to classes, the president had a change of heart. Large portions were "temporarily" roped off. It was promised that barriers would come down as soon as students became accustomed to using the established walks. (More than 30 years after College Heights opened, many of the "temporary" barriers were still in place.)

In spring, College of San Mateo blossomed with azaleas, rhododendrons and flowering Japanese plum trees. Thousands of blue-blooming *Lilies of the Nile*, agapanthus, cut from garden plots by San Mateo residents and donated to the college, were planted. Monterey pines created the campus perimeter. Occasional towering coast redwood trees highlighted lawns. In the canyon north of the Little Theater, gardeners working with head groundskeeper Ugo Paulazzo planted every known species of eucalyptus tree. In fall campus malls are strewn with fallen sycamore leaves.

College Heights landscaping won national acclaim. On Nov. 15, 1966, First Lady of the United States, Mrs. Lyndon Baines Johnson, presented the American Nurseryman's Association Award to College of San Mateo for its innovative gardens and overall landscape design. The award was accepted by Matt Fasanaro at a banquet at the Statler-Hilton in Washington, D.C.

The hilltop college was designed to be the ultimate modern educational institution. Keller and Gannon, a San Francisco consulting engineering firm, provided for maximum efficiency. Company electricians reported that the lighting system alone involved installation of a quarter million miles of wiring. On campus there were 14,600 fluorescent and mercury-vapor lamps in approximately 7,000 lighting fixtures.

Below ground were 15 miles of conduit for installation of the campus switchboard and its 260 telephones. The company also installed an 84 station fire alarm system and 165 electric clocks, each connected to a master clock which corrected its subordinate clocks once every 59 seconds.

Atop one classroom building was the college carillon, electric chimes provided by a cassette tape recorder played through an amplifier. These authentic-sounding chimes contributed to the collegiate ambiance. It was assumed they would be appreciated by all. When first played, Dean of Men William Walsh set the volume on high. "The bells could be heard for miles," remembered Walsh. One irate neighbor telephoned the president's office to ask: "Who do I talk to about dem damn bells." Thereafter, the carillons were carefully turned down.

College of San Mateo was recognized for its innovative landscaping. First Lady Mrs. Lyndon Baines Johnson presented the American Nurseryman's Association Award to Business Manager Matt Fasanaro.

As an administrator, Julio Bortolazzo was unique in the long history of College of San Mateo. From the time of his arrival on the Coyote Point campus, he became legendary. Dissatisfied with what he interpreted as a lack of college spirit, he had CSM decals printed and personally stopped arriving students, requesting that they place the decals in their car windows. Most did. At football games, everyone knew how to find the president; he was always in the stands on the 50-yard line.

Bortolazzo had a unique capacity for learning and remembering names. Probably no administrator in college history was more available to students or could address so many by name. He knew every person—faculty luminary, groundsman or engineer—who worked on campus and usually their spouses' names as well. Most responded with loyalty to him.

He enthusiastically engaged in dialogues with faculty members. During Coyote Point years, Bortolazzo ate lunch regularly with the Social Science Division, a practice he couldn't continue with the press of official business at College Heights.

Later in life, Bortolazzo commented that one of his biggest fears was that he would become an "illiterate administrator." He made time to read everything from astronomy to zoology, and frequently invited instructors into his office to discuss their courses and books they were requiring. For an instructor to receive a newspaper clipping, article or note from the president wasn't unusual.

Afternoon faculty meetings scheduled by Bortolazzo were religiously attended. He told instructors that such convocations "were not compulsory but neither were they optional." They got his message.

Julio Bortolazzo, a self-admitted workaholic, arrived on the campus by 6 a.m. daily and was usually the last to leave at the end of the day.

Bortolazzo was a self-admitted workaholic. A normal work day was 18 hours long. He never arrived on campus later than 6 a.m. Some subordinates became accustomed to being awakened by a ringing telephone anytime after 5 a.m. if the president wanted to discuss a new idea. Some never got accustomed to it. Connie Morse, wife of Phil Morse, recalled Bortolazzo awakening them just about every morning. Instructor Rudolph Lapp, then chair of the Social Science Division, remembered that Bortolazzo even called on Saturday or Sunday mornings. "If you want someone to tell you what he really thinks," stated Bortolazzo, "wake him up at dawn."

The president hated waiting. He had a buzzer system installed in each administrator's office so that he could summon subordinates at the press of a button. Instructor Douglas Crawford was frequently with Dean of Instruction Philip C. Garlington when the buzzer went off. "Garlington would go pale. It was a terrible thing to see, like God was calling…you'd see administrators rushing along the halls to line up outside Julio's office waiting to be admitted." Crawford told Garlington that being an administrator, and "going through the operation of having one's backbone removed," must be very painful.

Annoyed by Bortolazzo's infernal buzzing, Business Manager Fasanaro replaced the "irritating sound" device in his office with a gentle chime.

College telephone operator Louella Schaffley kept track of all administrators and key faculty members Bortolazzo might want to contact. "She developed a sixth sense and, no matter where on campus someone was, she'd find them," stated Phil Morse

Bortolazzo wasn't universally loved. A few found him dangerously intolerant. Some believed he was an egotist, grandstander and empire-builder who surrounded himself with lackeys and yes-men. One, who definitely wasn't, was Business Manager Matt Fasanaro, possessor of as volatile an Italian temper as Bortolazzo's. Their clashes, which often turned into nose-to-nose shouting matches, became fabled.

Nevertheless, Bortolazzo could be the ultimate charmer. Elected trustees fell victim to his magnetism and usually rubber-stamped his requests. After one meeting, a hostile and defeated trustee ungrammatically sighed: "It just don't do no good to talk to Julio."

At graduation in 1967, Bortolazzo presented an honorary degree to U.S. Navy aviator Dieter Dengler ('63), who had studied aviation at CSM. Dengler had been shot down while flying over Vietnam.

Captured by Viet Cong in 1966, he told the audience, he was dragged behind a water buffalo and hung upside down in the effort to make him sign statements against the United States. For a time he was tied to four stakes in the ground.

Dengler escaped from prison camp, detailing the flight in a book *Escaping from Laos*. For 23 days he crawled approximately 1,000 yards per day. He endured ants crawling on his body, leeches sucking his blood,…"and snakes, thousands of them."

Upon being honored at College of San Mateo, Dengler shared that dealing with the Viet Cong had been difficult, but nowhere near as difficult as dealing with Bortolazzo.

Dieter Dengler ('63), a pilot in the Vietnam war, spoke at graduation and was honored by the college in 1967.

In 1987, reflecting on his dozen years (1956-1968) as president, Bortolazzo would claim that they "were Camelot for me."

But times were invisibly changing.

The "college" as it was understood by most Americans—that is, class competitions, football games, campus queens, bonfires, pompon girls, sock hops and short hair—was rapidly disappearing. Soon colleges would become places unrecognized by those who'd long since graduated.

Traditions crumbled in the face of mounting student dissatisfaction. At College of San Mateo the yearbook, *The Campus*, for 40 years a student's most cherished memento of school days, was last published in 1961.

The 55-member Bulldog Marching Band, under the baton of music instructor Dick Crest, played a concert at Disneyland in 1963 and placed first as the best marching band in Northern California, competing at the Junior Rose Bowl in Pasadena. Smartly clad in elegant blue and white uniforms, the band for years had been a half time feature at College of San Mateo football games. In front of the group, during the 1960s, was majorette Judy Malone, holder of 95 baton twirling awards. "The last time the band took to the field was in 1966," stated new director Leo Bardes, "and it never went back." Students didn't want to be bothered with intricate marching steps. Thereafter, the band no longer wore the traditional uniforms, opting for blue blazers instead.

During the early years at College Heights, Homecoming was still the year's most important event. In 1965 Linda Fenger, a cosmetology student "holder of as many titles as a British field marshal," became Homecoming Queen. Two years later, Peggy Catheart, "a real eye popper," was crowned queen. A violinist in the orchestra and a pompon girl on the cheer leading staff, Catheart was the first African-American woman in the college's history to be so honored.

But by 1969, because of a general lack of interest, there was conjecture that Homecoming would soon become a thing of the past. The traditional bonfire at Coyote Point was canceled because of environmental regulations.

A couple of years later, student leaders were referring to Homecoming as that "annual farce" which the college holds onto because of some "foolish tradition." And as for the queen, the contest was regarded as an exercise for "chicken-feed minded females."

To run, it was pointed out, all any girl needed was a petition signed by 25 people. "No sweat if you're in something that shows off your finer attributes. Any girl can find 25 horny dudes in the cafeteria in about 10 minutes." The only thing the candidate gets, "besides possibly dying of embarrassment, is a freebie dinner…Whoopdegodamdoo." Editors of *The San Matean* were especially hard on the event: "Remember, only one girl comes out victorious. The rest go back to being dogs."

Students of the 1960s were a new breed. They were increasingly interested in social issues like civil rights, drug usage, women's causes, environmentalism, Communism, the draft and the war in Vietnam. By 1967, the Associated Women Students, an organization which had once specialized in genteel semi-annual teas, was discussing morality, social diseases, planned parenthood, abortion, and other "meaningful" topics.

The move from comfortable old Coyote Point to streamlined state of the art College Heights in 1963 seemed to be a catalyst which accelerated change. By the end of the decade, it was obvious that a revolution had taken place.

Faculty members slowly became aware of increasing student dissatisfaction on a variety of matters. Student grumbling, initially benign, later erupted into arguments which were vicious, violent and dangerously confrontational.

Many were less than jubilant about the move to the hilltop. Accustomed to the relaxed, rustic informality of Coyote Point, some returning students groused that the new concrete monolith had all the appeal of a giant mausoleum.

Matson Hall, the cafeteria at the Point where student and faculty alike enjoyed rap sessions around rustic wooden picnic tables, was replaced at College Heights with an antiseptically sterile facility many found "cold and impersonal." The dining area, some claimed, was "regimented like a prison." Bortolazzo responded that "the cafeteria isn't regimented; it's crowded." Still, administrators scrambled to rearrange furniture in an effort to make the place "more cozy."

Many found the student center and cafeteria at College Heights sterile and antiseptically pure, especially after the warmth and cozy atmosphere of Coyote Point.

The sterile appearance didn't last long. In a classic non sequitur, Dean of Men, William Walsh, responded by asking students not to put their feet on cafeteria walls. Bortolazzo toured the dining room and, finding hundreds of cigarette butts littering the floor, declared the place was a "disgrace."

Almost immediately, to placate students, trustees authorized an extension of the cafeteria. The addition, to the south above the historical museum, increased the facility's capacity from 600 to 1,300. (The cafeteria still proved inadequate. Construction of a small food service area at the northern end of the campus commenced in 1966.)

Students complained that cafeteria prices on the hilltop were higher than at Coyote Point and that food quality had declined.

Their annoyance level increased when, upon visiting the bookstore—the college's equivalent of a general store which sold everything from welding helmets to false hair pieces—students found, much to their anger, that *Playboy*, a publication always available to them at Coyote Point, hadn't made its way to College Heights. Ineffectively, they demanded that the magazine, which they praised for its literary content, be returned.

Bortolazzo delighted students with his oft repeated affirmation that College of San Mateo was "more than a high school with ashtrays." However, their irritation over the cafeteria and *Playboy* was compounded when Bortolazzo decreed that cigarette machines would not be permitted on the new campus. He said that this decision was based on the proven relationship between cigarette smoking and disease.

Bortolazzo was a hypocrite, said students. They pointed out that ashtrays and sand-filled buckets were found both around and inside classrooms.

Charles M. Devonshire, counselor and psychology instructor, sneered that the cigar-smoking Bortolazzo's action was "insulting to a mature student body." The editor of *The San Matean* wrote: "To ban all tobacco sales on campus, even in the bookstore, seems an action unbefitting a respectable collegiate institution. The announcement that CSM is the third California junior college to ban tobacco sales does nothing to add to its stature."

Though trustees upheld Bortolazzo's decision, the question of cigarette sales became a festering sore which occupied much of the president's energy for years. (In 1972, after Bortolazzo was gone, without fanfare, President Robert Ewigleben authorized installation of cigarette machines in the cafeteria.)

More troubling perhaps was the rise of student drug use during the 1960s. A survey in 1966 indicated that 23 percent of CSM students had used drugs at least once. Seven percent admitted to having experimented with LSD, a mind expanding substance not yet declared illegal. Lights were turned off in the Little Theater, Jan. 26, 1967, so students could listen to Dr. Richard Alpert discuss "The Psychedelic Revolution" to flickering candlelight amid the fragrance of sandlewood. While such statistics and behavior troubled many, psychologist Devonshire declared that "CSM students are no different from other students in America; they are doing what other people are doing in other places."

The San Matean ran advertisements headed: "Does LSD in sugar cubes spoil the taste of coffee?" Readers were encouraged to write Dr. Timothy Leary, Ph.D. for a long-playing record with the "facts about five levels of consciousness expansion."

Bortolazzo found himself on the defensive, attempting to downplay the growing numbers of stories of drugs on the campus. Reports were that marijuana was being smoked behind the library, just outside the cafeteria and in the parking lots. Although instructors later adamantly denied that such conversations had ever taken place, students openly discussed drug usage in class. The pungent smell of marijuana was often in hallways. Ken Costa ('69), editor of the campus newspaper, reported that it wasn't unusual for students to sit in the newsroom, passing a joint around.

In October 1967, Bortolazzo vehemently denied that marijuana could be purchased on campus. The same month two CSM students were arrested for possessing $100,000 worth of the weed.

Bortolazzo's inflexibility was a constant source of student dissatisfaction. At Coyote Point and later College Heights, the "Star-Spangled Banner" was played over the public address system each morning at 8 a.m. William Walsh,

Dean of Men (1958-1968), reported that every student on campus was expected to stop, stand at attention and face the flagpole. "Those in automobiles were required to turn off engines and step out of their cars." Violators were reported to the dean. Members of the Veterans Club became vigilantes, helping roundup non-participating "criminals." Often, said Walsh, "violators were required to attend club meetings for lectures on patriotism." For a first offense students got off with a lecture; a second violation resulted in suspension.

With the move to College Heights, the electric chimes blared out the National Anthem while Walsh personally raised the American flag. Band instructor Leo Bardes, at CSM starting in 1965, objected to the chimes, telling Bortolazzo that if such music was going to be done, it should be played right. Two weeks later the chimes were replaced by a tape recorded version of the "Star-Spangled Banner" played by the United States Marine Corps Band. "Hearing the first notes of the music, students ran toward the nearest building" to avoid participating, declared Bardes.

This ceremony, which went on until 1967, caused almost daily traffic snarls on access roads to the campus. That year, students in opposition to the American military involvement in Southeast Asia refused to participate further in the ritual. A combination of anti-war student activism and intolerable traffic tangles brought the solemn ceremony to an end.

The campus dress code, rules established in the late 1950s at Coyote Point, became a focal point of further student agitation. Editors of *The San Matean* found the regulations "absurd and antiquated." (Previously, students had been merely admonished to dress "appropriately.")

The dean of men explained in 1966: "The purpose of a campus dress code is to encourage students to attire themselves in a manner in keeping with the serious academic intent of the college. Somehow the students' frame of mind is related to how they're dressed…they don't cavort in the pools when properly attired."

"The purpose of a campus dress code is to encourage students to attire themselves in a manner in keeping with the serious academic intent of the college." Students don't "cavort in the pools when properly attired," stated Dean Bill Walsh in 1966.

Changing times resulted in different student values. Dean of Men William Walsh and Dean of Women Ruth Weston found themselves in the uncomfortable position of attempting to enforce rules which students found silly and archaic.

According to the code, males were required to wear full length trousers, shoes and socks. Bermuda shorts on campus were unthinkable. For women, "appropriate dress means street length dresses or skirts and sweaters and blouses. Skating skirts, shorts, slacks and other beach or active sports attire are not acceptable on campus." Student editors lambasted the absurdity of the regulations. "If shoulders are shrugged at short-short skirts, a rule forbidding women from wearing properly fitting slacks on a cold day is sheer mania." Both men and women were warned that "thongs, sock shoes, slippers and bare feet are also cause for ejection" from class.

Those who refused to conform were turned in by the faculty to respective deans, either Bill Walsh or Dean of Women Ruth Weston. Sociology instructor Irving Witt remembered one woman student who went to a ceramics class wearing slacks. The instructor sent her to Weston who in turn asked her to leave campus and return only when appropriately attired. Bortolazzo was constantly calling Walsh to tell him to nab some student wearing shorts. Walsh stated that there was approximately one student turned in a day.

Finally, much to the consternation of administrators, April 6, 1966, the Student Council unanimously liberalized the dress code permitting capris (later defined as slacks) for women and Bermuda shorts for men. Appropriate footwear was still required. Even student body president Abelardo Doctolero ('66) agreed with Bortolazzo that "bare feet are obnoxious."

Faced with the reality that his conservative viewpoint wouldn't prevail, Bortolazzo reluctantly signed the new code but only after student leaders, while attacking him as being "contemptuous" of their action, agreed that the president's "recommendations" could be published along with the relaxed rules. He reiterated the old code, underscoring that "slacks for women and shorts for men…are of extremely dubious suitability for education…this is my way of looking at it. I am confident it will be your way too."

Students weren't alone in being forced to conform to a dress code. Women faculty were required to wear dresses or suits with nylons *and* a girdle. Instructor Jean Wirth, hired to teach English in 1958, remembered that her division director, Stanley Sharp, "used to rub up against me about once a week to be sure I was wearing the girdle."

Maintaining decorum of an earlier age was a losing battle. As late as 1971, coaches in the college's Athletic Department found themselves attempting to preserve old-time traditions. The "disgusting trend" toward long hair, side-burns, mustaches and beards was more than they were willing to tolerate. A 1969 unanimous ruling by the coaches was abundantly clear—no facial hair; sideburns no lower than the bottom of the ear; hair neatly trimmed back.

Five members of the track team, including the 1969-1970 most valuable runner, were barred from competing because of long hair. The runners said "no" to barbers. "We are men and we feel that we should be treated like men."

College President David Mertes, a one-time zoology professor, called for a moratorium on the regulation and asked Athletic Director Herb Hudson (a member of the faculty since 1947 and director since 1964) to reinstate the runners.

Hudson was obdurate. Long hair, he said, would lead to the destruction of sports programs. Declaring that the administration lacked the experience to deal with athletes, he steadfastly refused to alter his directive barring the offensive runners.

Faced with this embarrassing stalemate, the normally even-tempered Mertes ordered removal of Hudson as Athletic Director. The trackmen were reinstated.

David Mertes, CSM's president from 1971-1978, first came to the college as an instructor of zoology in 1965. Later he headed the Life Science Division. Becoming president after a decade of change and upheaval, Mertes was a much needed stabilizing influence.

During the 1960s, not only did the new college have all the appearances architecturally of a big college or university, it also became a cultural center and an arena for social and political change.

Big name entertainment groups converged on San Mateo. The Smothers Brothers, a comedy team specializing in satire, packed the Men's Gymnasium March 17, 1964. College students and people from the community listened to an evening of folk songs served up with ample doses of political and social commentary in a program entitled "Think Ethnic."

The New Christy Minstrels, a singing group, invaded the campus April 21, 1964 with hand-clapping, foot-stomping rhythm. The next month, Louis 'Satchmo' Armstrong occupied the gymnasium to wow an audience of almost 3,000 ranging in age from little children to senior citizens.

The place "rocked and roared" for more than three hours while Armstrong demonstrated ever so clearly that "jazz was far from dead." This appreciative audience didn't want to go home. Armstrong did five encores—all of them his latest hit "Hello Dolly." Duke Ellington appeared in October and The Four Preps sang in November.

Dec. 1, 1964, an unbroken line of automobiles extended from the Bayshore freeway to the college campus. Every parking space was taken. Bortolazzo managed to drive onto campus and asked a security guard, attempting to direct traffic, what was going on. "Some guy named *Bobby Deelin* is singing in the gym."

Bob Dylan, a sloppy and disheveled boy from Minnesota whose music had already shaken up the nation, captured his audience at CSM with a rare combination of talent and philosophy. Some thought of him as a "mysterious guitar-strumming hillbilly." He was famed for his protest ballads concerned with bombs and racial prejudice.

Backers of the CSM concert series were overwhelmed with his drawing power. "Dylan is more than a performer to those who follow him and his words." His is "a new voice for a new generation" that is "at once frustrating and refreshing," wrote Skip Curley ('66), reporter for *The San Matean*. Social commentators declared that Dylan—poet, folk singer and individualist—was the most important writer of folk songs in decades. He "speaks for the whole lost crowd."

In one very important respect, Dylan differed from parents, college professors and, for that matter, other entertainers of his ilk. At College Heights, as wherever he sang in America, Dylan appeared to be talking *to* the packed audience, not *at* them. Perhaps appropriately, the entertainer-philosopher opened his CSM program with "The Times They are A Changin."

Entertainer Merv Griffin, who'd briefly attended San Mateo Junior College during the 1940s before going on to fame and fortune in television, returned

Of all the entertainers who performed at CSM, perhaps Bob Dylan, who appeared in December 1964, had the greatest appeal. His became the voice for the new generation.

to the campus Dec. 13, 1965. Griffin packed the Little Theater to record his network television show with special guest Carol Channing who was then closing her San Francisco run of "Hello Dolly." This was the first time that the Griffin Show had moved en masse from its New York base.

Excited admirers waved placards reading "Merv for President" and "San Mateo is Proud of You." The town mayor made him an honorary citizen of San Mateo, an honor Griffin noted which was rather special "since I was born here."

The home-town boy briefly reminisced about his junior college days. Once, detailed to line up entertainment for a college assembly, he hired two scantily clad exotic dancers from San Francisco's Tenderloin. "The girls didn't go over well with the president's wife [Carlena Morris], and that was the last time I was ever entertainment chairman."

Griffin returned in 1978 to record a program at the campus television station for the benefit of telecommunications students.

College Heights became a marketplace of ideas and intellectual expression. Between 1963 and 1969, few weeks went by without a student debate, rap session or lecture to generate thinking. Bortolazzo's years were characterized by a constant stream of speakers on campus. Long-haired poet Allen Ginsberg, the bearded prophet of 'hip' and perhaps the liveliest speaker to appear, stirred up the campus with 75 minutes of Buddhist chants and philosophic prose in November 1965. Ginsberg left many CSM students in shock through his frank discussion of his mental and sexual experiences, exploring them in such a way as to make listeners look honestly and unashamedly at themselves.

The Right Rev. Joseph T. McGucken, the Roman Catholic Archbishop of San Francisco, spoke in the Little Theater in February 1966. Professor David M. Potter, chairman of the history department at Stanford University, contributed to the intellectual cauldron in March 1966, with his lecture entitled "Conformity and Dissent in the American Character." In May 1966, African-American comedian Dick Gregory, introduced to students by young black San Francisco Assemblyman Willie Brown, condemned the war in Vietnam. Erich Fromm, noted author and psychologist best known for his book *The Art of*

San Francisco Assemblyman Willie Brown introduced a number of black speakers to College of San Mateo during the 1960s.

Loving, spoke to a standing room only crowd the next week (Oct. 14, 1964) on "Narcissism, Group Fixation and Prejudice."

During the spring of 1964, former presidential press secretary Pierre Salinger, then hoping to become the Democratic Party's candidate for the U.S. Senate, faced students in the Outdoor Theater. He told them how near the United States had come to World War III during the Kennedy years—looking down the barrel of the "nuclear gun" in the Cuban missile crisis.

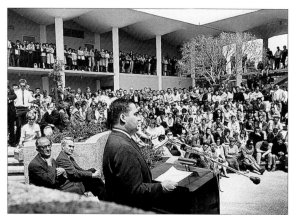

Students thronged the amphitheater in spring of 1964 to listen to Senate-candidate Pierre Salinger. Formerly press secretary for John F. Kennedy, Salinger maintained rapt attention by evoking the memory of Kennedy. Seated behind Salinger were Julio Bortolazzo and Social Science Division chairman Rudolph Lapp.

Though Barry Goldwater, the conservative Republican presidential hopeful in 1964, and his high-powered entourage arrived on campus an hour late, Bortolazzo was at the podium in the gymnasium to introduce the candidate on April 15, after which a group of smiling, cowboy-hatted "Goldwater Girls" attempted to generate enthusiasm by leading a chorus of "Welcome Barry."

Ronald Reagan's campaign swept in on a Saturday in 1966. Even so, approximately 1,000 (mostly non-students) came out to hear the gubernatorial candidate along with a number of other Republican hopefuls. Reagan chose this venue to discuss the faculty of the University of California and its drift toward politics. (In February 1967, CSM students joined a 5,000-person march to Sacramento sponsored by the California Federation of Teachers, in opposition to Governor Reagan's proposed cut in the budget of California's higher education system and the imposition of a tuition fee for University of California and state college students.)

As early as 1965, with an ever-increasing number of Americans being sent to Vietnam, there was a great awakening of interest in American involvement in Southeast Asia. Students questioned national policy and grew increasingly uneasy about being drafted.

Local politician Paul "Pete" McCloskey, a former Marine Corps officer and then a liberal Republican seeking a seat in Congress, spoke on campus in 1967 and again in 1968. He won student support, calling for a lowering of the voting age from 21 to 18 and by lining up against the Lyndon Johnson

Vietnam policy. "Every fact coming out of Vietnam is colored to justify the administration's position. It is designed to couch the facts in order to indicate progress."

Students crowded the Little Theater in October 1968, to hear presidential hopeful Dr. Benjamin Spock harangue them about poverty, racial tensions, poor educational facilities and Vietnam. He declared that the war was immoral and illegal and couldn't be won. The baby-doctor turned politician declared that the United States was using "all the illegal laws of warfare, poisoning crops, destroying civilian dwellings, placing civilians in concentration camps and bombing non-strategic targets."

Conservative Republican presidential candidate Barry Goldwater faced CSM students during his 1964 campaign.

Philip C. Garlington, reflecting on his long professional relationship with Julio Bortolazzo, stated that wherever Bortolazzo went during his academic career, his campuses were dedicated to free speech. "There were always public forums, pro and con, about race and Communism, sometimes to the distress of a community's more conservative citizens."

Even while College of San Mateo was still at Coyote Point, in 1962, Bortolazzo ruffled the county's conservative feathers by sponsoring a four session program: "Communism…the Challenge and the Answer."

In 1964, with the unanimous approval of Bortolazzo and the board of trustees, students invited Albert "Mickey" Lima, chairman of the Communist Party of Northern California, to speak during the activities hour on April 30.

No issue in years had so excited and interested the people of the Peninsula. This was an era of confrontation. Conservative residents questioned Bortolazzo's patriotism. H. Richard O'Hara, Hillsborough chairman of the California Department, Military Order of the World Wars Americanism Committee, blasted the appearance of a Communist on campus. "As a taxpayer, I think the officials of the school should get down to the business of teaching academic subjects rather than playing politics with our student body." The San Mateo County American Legion, of which Bortolazzo was a member, engaged in

Thomas Lantos, a professor of economics from San Francisco State University, frequently spoke at College Heights during the 1960s.

wordy debate and withdrew a speaking invitation because Bortolazzo had allowed a Communist to speak on campus. The president had addressed the American Legion at its annual luncheon for five of the past six years.

Veteran Assemblyman Louis Francis, archenemy of Communism and subversion in California, lampooned Bortolazzo. "I am surprised that this program was approved for so-called academic freedom, but it actually gives the opportunity to this top Communist leader to attempt to indoctrinate and inculcate our students at a tax-supported institution."

"I won't retreat one step on this issue," the college president shot back. He added that he'd never seen a student converted to any point of view by listening to a presentation by a speaker. He declared further that Lima would be no more successful in converting the students than was Hugh Fine, coordinator of the John Birch Society, when he had recently spoken for three hours on the principles of the extreme right.

Instead of backing down, Bortolazzo eloquently defended the principles of free speech and, moreover, invited Lima to return to College of San Mateo, this time to debate San Francisco State College economics professor Tom Lantos. The topic, "Is Communism Good for the United States," was debated in the college gymnasium, May 5, 1964. It was attended by approximately 3,000.

The audience, feeling that Lima offered a weak argument, jeered him while applauding Lantos. The visiting professor began by stating that "the function of higher education is not to make ideas safe for students, but to make the students safe for ideas." Newspapers headlined that Lantos' was an "awesome triumph." At the conclusion of the debate, musical strains of "America" wafted across campus from the loud speakers of the electric chimes. "So much of Bortolazzo," stated Professor Michael Kimball, "was pure theater."

Bortolazzo was delighted with both the event and the outcome. He proudly told reporters: "I have one of the most enlightened colleges in America on the evils of Communism."

Nevertheless, the *San Mateo Times* railed against him. The editorial writer's front-page blast not only attacked Bortolazzo but wondered if voters had known what direction the college would take, whether they would have approved the recent multi-million dollar bond issue resulting in the new campus. Several days after the debate, the topic was still so controversial, the *Times* devoted an entire page to reader response.

College of San Mateo continued to be a public forum, a marketplace for ideas of all types. More than 2,000 students gathered in December 1965, to partake in a debate between Bortolazzo and Bettina Aptheker, the 21-year old leader of the University of California Free Speech Movement and an admitted Communist. She was the daughter of Herbert Aptheker, the acknowledged leading theoretician of the Communist Party in the United States.

"This government has conducted witch-hunts and executed and imprisoned its victims. It is time to affirm the right to be a Communist, the right of Communists to speak and act, and the right of the American people to listen and think for themselves," declared the young Miss Aptheker, a history major at Berkeley.

Bortolazzo bested Aptheker on all fronts. He declared that her tactics "spread distrust, dismay and disgust far beyond the borders of the Berkeley campus." He continued: "We value our heritage of free speech, but your problems, Miss Aptheker, are not our problems and your methods are not ours. What went on at the University of California has no place at the College of San Mateo."

S.I. Hayakawa, later elected to the U.S. Senate from California, participated in a Community Education program at the new campus in 1964.

Race was unquestionably the paramount social topic of the 1960s. On July 2, 1964, President Lyndon Baines Johnson signed the Civil Rights Act. This outlawed discrimination in hotels and other public accommodations. Literary tests for voting were now required in writing. Anyone who had finished the sixth grade was deemed literate. The government was now prepared to bring suit against school boards for racial segregation. This was the most far-reaching civil rights policy ever enacted.

The next year Dr. Martin Luther King Jr. began a voter registration drive to enroll three million African Americans throughout the South.

But in the midst of this series of successes, the civil rights movement began to fragment. One off-shoot was the Black Power crusade. Frustration in

Watts, a mostly black neighborhood of Los Angeles, exploded in riot during the summer of 1965. Before the flames were out 34 people had died, thousands were in jail and property damage ran into the millions.

Julio Bortolazzo was deeply impressed by the civil rights movement and genuinely troubled by the plight of African-American students. In 1965, of the approximately 8,000 daytime students enrolled at College of San Mateo, only 87 were black. Counselors estimated that of this number approximately 90 percent dropped or flunked out by the end of the year. Among minority students in Redwood City and East Palo Alto, CSM had the reputation of a "flunk out school."

"If we in the junior colleges are to offer a real chance for success to the disadvantaged student, our traditional open door is not enough…our eyes must be opened to recognize the problems which far too often have turned our open door into a revolving door," stated Bortolazzo.

He continued that it was "utterly ridiculous" that a nation as great as the United States could not find a way to help lift the culturally deprived "out of the cycle of poverty which presently traps them." Bortolazzo asked the faculty: "What should we be doing to prevent the outbreak of the type of desperate violence which the riots in Watts represent?"

In an effort to put the brake on the revolving door, Bortolazzo became the impetus behind development of the College Readiness Program (CRP). It began in summer of 1966. The program was under the leadership of English instructor and counselor Jean Wirth.

"Julio was willing to take risks," stated Wirth. A recruitment program was undertaken in East Palo Alto. "We zeroed in on poor black kids who hadn't done well in high school and who had no intention of going to college," added Wirth.

Space for the College Readiness Program was found in the unventilated basement of the college's Administration Building. The program was later moved to the complete opposite end of the campus and shared a building with horticulture.

"We began changing the color of the campus," stated Wirth. Student tutors, many willing to work 12 hours a day, were hired. Interestingly, about

Initially, Julio Bortolazzo's appeal to the faculty for assistance in creating a program for disadvantaged minority students, brought limited response. English instructor Jean Wirth accepted the challenge and became founder of the College Readiness Program.

50 percent of the tutors, mostly white, had themselves failed somewhere along the way. Many had long hair and more traditional CSM faculty sarcastically referred to them simply as "Beatniks." Nevertheless, they worked with minority students on a one-to-one basis. Recruits into the program were taught new concepts of school, how to read and how to study. One of the biggest problems was overcoming the neighborhood attitude that it was "not cool" to study.

"During that first summer when students didn't show up, tutors jumped in their cars and went out to find them and bring 'em in," reported Wirth.

New students were full of admiration for the program which included classes in English and reading along with counseling and guidance. "They make you study. I was trying to write everything down. They taught me to take notes," said one obviously admiring student.

College of San Mateo's Readiness Program was unique in the United States in that it was not controlled by any government agency. It was a single college attempting to deal with the "revolving door." Bortolazzo was emphatic that this was a must program. "Either these people have an opportunity to obtain an education and become productive members of society, or society must take the consequences," he stated in 1966.

It was an expensive program. College trustees put up an initial $10,000. Another $10,000 was received through a federal work-study program.

Donations poured in from the private sector. Sizable gifts were received from the San Mateo Foundation, the Lucie Stern Foundation and the Guy F. Atkinson Foundation. Philanthropists David Packard and Daniel Koshland were staunch supporters of the Readiness Program—both morally and financially. Participants in the program received free bus transportation between East Palo Alto and the campus, free lunches, a few hours of work a day and daily tutoring sessions.

College leaders were ecstatic about initial results of the program. "We started the summer with 40 students and expected to finish with five," stated Wirth. "But when the class finished we still had 39." Thirty-six of them enrolled for the fall semester.

Philanthropist Daniel Koshland was a dominating influence on the Citizen's Committee which recommended construction of College Heights and later provided leadership in the successful bond drive. After 1966, he contributed heavily to the College Readiness Program. A grateful college awarded him an honorary associate of arts degree.

Dynamic and charismatic Robert Hoover was appointed by Julio Bortolazzo to head the College Readiness Program.

Success of the program attracted new minority students. Many Asian and Latin American students along with 200 African Americans had enrolled by fall 1966. In February 1967, there were 300. Many were being helped by the program but about half chose College of San Mateo "because they have been encouraged seeing how Negroes are treated here," stated Eric Gattman, coordinator of the College Readiness Program. "Instead of waiting for them to come to us, the college went to them and offered them inducements to attend."

"This program takes any black student who wants to go to college…and we'll do whatever is necessary to keep him there. If he needs transportation, we'll provide it. If he needs money, we'll try to find it…If he has personal problems, we'll counsel with him. If he's having academic difficulty, we'll tutor him. If he's in jail, we'll make bail. But there's one unbroken rule: he must do college-level work…Black students, like all students, frequently live up to the highest expectations set for them," stated Jean Wirth about the College Readiness Program.

Wirth, a six foot-five inch Caucasian, often shocked those white students who volunteered to tutor. "We don't want any tutors who come with the 'white missionary' syndrome. They are not in this to help poor black people; they're in this to learn."

Bortolazzo and Wirth fully understood that the program could not, and should not, long survive under the leadership of a white woman. After a search, the president offered the position to Robert Hoover, 35, an East Palo Alto community leader. The charismatic Hoover, a great admirer of the program, declared that "CSM has made the biggest stride of any college in the area, four-year or junior, in the field of recruiting and keeping minority students in college." Hoover came aboard Sept. 1, 1967. Thereafter Wirth was listed as the program's supervisor and Bob Hoover was the director.

Across the nation during the summer of 1966, more than 40 American cities experienced racial unrest. Racial tension mounted almost daily. College of San Mateo appeared to be one of the rare places where attempts were being made to deal with racial inequalities.

In 1967, Peggy Catheart, an African-American woman and CSM pom-pon girl, was elected Homecoming Queen. She was the first black to receive this honor in the history of the college.

Black students trusted Julio Bortolazzo. He often visited the CRP office to help relieve tensions by discussing campus difficulties. When minority students were especially upset about a matter, they knew his door was open and that he would not only listen but take action if at all possible. But Bortolazzo, after a disagreement with the board of trustees, resigned in March 1968.

The new president, announced on May 10, 1968, was 39-year old Robert L. Ewigleben, a native of Michigan and former dean of administrative affairs at Humboldt State College near Eureka. Readiness Program participants quickly came to believe that Ewigleben wasn't sympathetic to their cause. He appeared indifferent and perhaps oblivious to racial tension on campus. Ewigleben never visited the College Readiness Program office. Distraught students found him too busy to talk.

Meanwhile the dynamic Bob Hoover continued doing his job well. He recruited blacks off the streets and out of pool halls and even jails. Students were not exclusively drawn from local neighborhoods. The program's fame had rapidly spread. In small groups, African-American students from across the country headed toward San Mateo. The Readiness Program came to be watched carefully by increasingly suspicious federal authorities.

Sally Smith, an African American born in San Mateo, a graduate of San Mateo High School and one of the first to be recruited into the Readiness Program, recalled that about eight students drove west from Chicago in a "big old black gangster-type Cadillac limousine." Other groups came from Kansas, New York and New Jersey. Still others arrived from the Deep South. Perhaps as many as 200 students were from outside California.

By fall of 1968, when Ewigleben became president, there were approximately 1,000 minority students. This included many people of color—Mexican Americans, Native Americans, Samoans and Puerto Ricans. Approximately 650 were black.

College photographer Isago Tanaka recorded day-to-day progress of students in the College Readiness Program. After the racial upheavals of 1968, Tanaka hid prints and negatives fearing they would be seized by police attempting to implicate participants. Tanaka said he destroyed the pictures. The poignant collection, however, quite by accident, was found in 1996.

"We were all so excited and so full of hope," stated English professor Jeanne Angier. Sally Smith, who was saved from flunking out of CSM when Jean Wirth started the CRP and later graduated with honors from Mills College, agreed: "There were many people of color; it was a dynamic campus."

Changes in the College of San Mateo as a result of the CRP weren't hard to find. It had taken on the genuine appearance of a "people's college." In 1968, for the first time, 38 black students successfully transferred to four-year institutions. CSM's 360 instructors now included 11 blacks, eight of them new in the fall of 1968. Black history and literature along with a number of other black oriented courses had been added to the curriculum. Many old school instructors felt threatened by the number of black faces on campus.

Inflammatory racial rhetoric continued to stir up emotions on campus throughout the decade. Black writer Louis Lomax, whose books included *The Reluctant African* and *The Negro Revolt*, had spoken Oct. 7, 1964, on "The Chain of Prejudice." Voted by *Ebony* magazine as one of the 100 most influential men in America, he told a largely white audience in the gymnasium that "the problem with the American white man is that he has been doing wrong for so long and getting away with it that he now believes he is doing right."

Lomax concluded his presentation by telling the hushed audience: "I only hope the white man learns to love before the Negro learns to hate." The speaker received a standing ovation.

April 4, 1968, Dr. Martin Luther King Jr., the non-violent black leader of the civil rights movement, was cut down by an assassin's bullet when he stepped onto the balcony of a Memphis, Tennessee, motel. In the wake of his death, riots erupted in a score of American cities.

The same month, at College of San Mateo, San Francisco State College instructor Jimmy Garret spoke to increasingly agitated and nervous students during the college's first Black Culture Week. It was a genuine attempt to get white students to understand the black position. Garret warned that "there is going to be a racial war in this country."

Also in April, Bobby Seale, spokesman for the Black Panther Self Defense Party, addressed a predominantly white audience in the college's Little Theater. He warned that they could expect violence during the summer of 1968. He urged black listeners to arm and prepare to defend themselves. Other members of the Black Panthers spoke to CRP students on campus.

College officials in the spring were concerned enough about the possibility of violence that San Mateo County police officers who were attending classes were asked not to bring sidearms onto campus.

Soft-spoken Robert Ewigleben, apparently overwhelmed by day-to-day college problems, and, it would seem, unaware of the magnitude of racial tension not only on his own campus but across the nation, totally ignored the Readiness Program. Until October, when frustration bubbled over into trouble, he neither responded to calls nor answered letters from the CRP office. Ewigleben had never met program founder and supervisor Jean Wirth.

By October 1968, the Readiness Program was allegedly in trouble. Jobs promised to participating students didn't materialize. Many were forced to withdraw. "Demands" for support were made on the trustees, who both rejected the terminology and moved slowly. "We have not moved far enough or fast enough," Hoover told trustees.

President Ewigleben responded publicly. Addressing the campus via closed-circuit television on KCSM-TV in October, he admitted that the Readiness Program had not had the support of the academic community. Race, he declared, was "an even more important problem than this damnable war we're involved in." He promised full support of the CRP.

There was no lack of financial support for the CRP. The Department of Education offered a $105,000 federal grant. Acceptance was contingent on the college raising an equal amount in matching funds. In spite of substantial support pledges from the private sector, College of San Mateo never moved to make this a reality. Francis Pearson, President of the Board of Trustees, declared support for the CRP from that governing body but not before he conferred with faculty and administrative leaders.

Nationally known black writer Louis Lomax told CSM students in 1964: "I only hope the white man learns to love before the Negro learns to hate."

Within the CRP, frustration mounted. Students, faced with reduced support, regarded it as a threat to their ability to attend college at all. Some felt that because they had been actively recruited into the program, the college had a responsibility to place success within their grasp.

There was a San Mateo version of black power. Throughout the CRP experiment there was a militant, strident tone, one which offended many faculty members and trustees. But there was no violence. In an article published in the *Southern Education Report* (November 1968), Jean Wirth emphasized: "Violence comes only when there is no other route. We've found other routes. We have more important things to do."

Robert Ewigleben (center) became CSM's president in the fall of 1968. Within hours, racial tension turned to violence. The young president felt under siege and unable to cope with the growing crisis.

Student anger and frustration finally surfaced Tuesday, Oct. 16, 1968, when minorities, mainly black, invaded the college's Administration Building. A nervous Ewigleben alerted police.

Helmeted officers and sheriff's deputies swarmed onto campus and into the building. After some impromptu negotiation conducted by counselor Allan Brown—a tense drama which was filmed and later that day shown coast-to-coast on the Huntley-Brinkley Report, the nation's leading television news program—police withdrew. However at 5 p.m. when students remained in the building, 75 law enforcement officers were called in and the building cleared. There were no injuries or arrests.

This confrontation made headlines. Hoover, a strong supporter of student demands, declared that the action had been taken to show displeasure with the administration and trustees for failing to address minority needs.

"Fun and games are over," a visibly shaken Ewigleben told students the next day. The "strongest measures" would be taken to prevent recurrences. Further protests wouldn't be tolerated. "Police have been alerted."

An uneasy calm settled over the campus amid promises that problems would be worked out. On November 1, Philip C. Garlington, acting superintendent, suspended Hoover from his position at the Readiness Program, allegedly for failure to implement trustee directives. Students and many faculty members were enraged. Ewigleben reinstated Hoover four days later.

Meanwhile, on November 19, San Francisco State University was closed after confrontations between students and police. Rioting there revolved around race and the war in Vietnam. Denied access to their campus, many of these protestors now appeared at College of San Mateo, exacerbating the general nervous state of affairs.

On December 12, in a matter completely unrelated to the Readiness Program, after being denied access to a campus bathroom by a maintenance person, a black student complained to Robert Ewigleben, ultimately striking him. Police who were summoned swept onto campus in full riot gear. When the student was detained in the president's office, a plate-glass window separating the office from the hallway was smashed.

The same day College Readiness students staged a rally calling for a class boycott. Kenneth Cheeseman, 20, a white student from Belmont who was annoyed and disgusted by the ongoing rhetoric, pulled wires from the public address system. He was beaten by angry listeners, his jaw broken.

On Friday, December 13, at a noontime rally, Readiness Program students took almost two hours to present their case for improved minority education. At 1:45 p.m. talk was forgotten and frustrated students began a rampage of mindless violence.

Authorities estimated that between 150 and 800 raced through classroom buildings shouting "strike, strike, strike." Furniture was bashed against walls and sand-filled ashtrays thrown down halls.

In a collective frenzy, demonstrators, both black and white, heaved chairs through glass doors and broke countless windows with rocks and pipes. A San Jose television crew was savagely attacked and beaten; its camera was smashed.

Student John Matthews, bruised and bleeding, told reporters "I was beaten up pretty badly and had reason to fear for my life." He was struck with a pipe and pounded by fists. Three electronics instructors—Stan Scott, George Angerbauer and Lorne MacDonald—were attacked by militants. Several students were injured, a few seriously. One girl was pushed down a flight of stairs, landing on a pile of broken glass.

Students were stunned by the frenzy of destruction by rioters. Hundreds of windows and glass doors were smashed.

On several occasions, embattled Robert Ewigleben summoned police. In the process he transformed the campus into a virtual fortress.

Strikers wearing red arm bands entered the offices of *The San Matean*. Five typewriters were destroyed, one window to the outside was shattered and the glass cubicle around the adviser's officer was smashed.

Within 30 minutes, club-wielding police surged onto campus. By then, most militants had faded away.

"There will be no more rallies," fumed the embattled Ewigleben. "Violence will not be tolerated." Students returning for Monday classes found the campus occupied by 400 uniformed policemen. Sentries manned roadblocks on access roads to campus and checked student identifications. Morning traffic was backed up along the Nineteenth Avenue Freeway to El Camino Real. The club-wielding, masked and helmeted San Francisco Police Department Tactical Squad executed drills on the lawn outside the College Readiness Program offices. A police helicopter whirled overhead.

This massive police presence, which ultimately involved every department on the peninsula, including the California Highway Patrol, continued until the Christmas break (December 19) and resumed when classes began anew in January. The police occupation cost College of San Mateo $20,000 a day.

Early in the morning of Jan. 7, 1969, CSM dean of instruction Philip C. Garlington and his wife were awakened by the sound of gun shots at their San Mateo home. Upon investigating, Garlington narrowly escaped death when a firebomb, apparently tossed through a garage window, exploded.

The garage became an inferno. Flames destroyed two cars and invaded the master bedroom. Damage to the house ran into the tens of thousands of dollars.

Arsonists, identified and pursued by the FBI, were not associated either with College of San Mateo or the Readiness Program.

"The administration has no wish to indict the College Readiness Program for this violence," declared John Hubbard of CSM's public relations office, "but there is ample evidence that the violence was planned, and also that many who are not students here participated." He noted that some cars in the parking lots bore San Francisco State College stickers. Outside agitators became the college's official position.

Nevertheless, within 24 hours of the riot Ewigleben had taken steps to dismantle the Readiness Program. "Effective immediately," in letters dated December 16, Ewigleben removed both Hoover and Wirth from their positions. They were ordered to clear out their offices and be completely off campus by 8 a.m. the next morning, December 17. Wirth and Hoover firmly believe that had Bortolazzo still been president, there would never have been a riot. (Later Hoover was offered a new position, away from students, working with the chancellor-superintendent. The next year Wirth was reassigned to teach English, but it was her understanding that a condition of her reemployment was that, "I was never to be allowed to speak with a black student." She concluded that this made her future at College of San Mateo absolutely impossible.)

A distressed Bill Somerville, fellow with the Wright Institute in Berkeley and, after 1974, director of the San Mateo Foundation, wrote (Dec. 17, 1968) to then Chancellor Clifford G. Erickson. He referred to the College of San Mateo's Readiness Program as having been the "most ambitious and best organized program in the United States." Somerville stated that Hoover and Wirth had developed "what I found to be the most comprehensive counseling and tutoring effort found on any two or four-year campus in the country." Somerville was blatantly critical of Ewigleben's uncertain leadership.

Because he so thoroughly believed in the CRP, philanthropist-executive David Packard, later assistant secretary of defense during the Richard M. Nixon presidency, offered $25,000 if Hoover and Wirth were rehired. Philanthropist Jean Weaver, an heir of the Proctor and Gamble fortune (frequently associated with Peninsula Community Foundation), promised another $50,000. These offers were not accepted.

How the December 13 rioting began has never been determined. Agents of the Federal Bureau of Investigation on campus the day of the upheaval later claimed that Stanford University Professor H. Bruce Franklin had been among the demonstrators. Some on the faculty were convinced that Franklin had spoken on campus the day before. This cannot be documented. The FBI

Four-hundred riot police, including the San Francisco Police Department Tactical Squad, occupied College Heights in December 1968. Angry administrators and trustees blamed outside agitators for the upheaval. Nevertheless, the successful College Readiness Program was methodically dismantled.

believed that Franklin was financing student violence with monies funneled to him from Communist China.

Jean Wirth, who never returned to College of San Mateo, was in her office at the time of the riot. Because of the office's isolation, she was unaware that the upheaval was going on. She admitted that many had come to expect violence but does not believe CRP students had been responsible.

Sally Smith, who became a consultant and a specialist in development training for non-profit organizations, stated that many students came to believe that the breaking of the first window, which ignited the violence, may well have been done by a federal agent.

Years later, after passage of the Freedom of Information Act, many former Readiness Program students, including Sally Smith, learned that undercover agents had been recording their activities on campus since the advent of the program during the summer of 1966. Smith stated that her FBI file was "extensive."

By the beginning of the spring semester 1969, the nature of the College of San Mateo campus had changed again. During winter break, Hoover and Wirth worked tirelessly to place scores of promising black students in other colleges and universities across the nation. Most didn't officially transfer; they simply didn't come back to College of San Mateo.

Many, reported Sally Smith, returned to their neighborhoods and never attended college again—anywhere. Still others wanted to continue their quest for education but had not achieved the level of academic sophistication necessary for success.

For these students, Hoover and Wirth worked to create Nairobi College in East Palo Alto. Nairobi, a further effort to stop the academic revolving door, was a direct result of San Mateo's Readiness Program and the December debacle. In less than six months, Wirth raised almost $1 million for the pioneer project. Much of the money came from wealthy private contributors, the likes of David Packard and San Francisco philanthropist Daniel Koshland, who avidly believed in the value of the project.

Black students who remained at College of San Mateo never talked about what happened, stated Sally Smith. "The college rapidly went back to being white."

Business instructor Lois A. Callahan, new on campus in 1968, stated that after the upheaval was over the faculty "just didn't discuss it. We just went back to business as usual."

Within a semester much of the progress made since 1966 had been lost and CSM was reverting to its pre-Readiness Program reputation as a "flunk out" school for minorities. "They were beaten down and," stated English instructor Jean Angiers, "student apathy set in."

The gut wrenching upheavals signaled a change in Ewigleben's leadership. In early 1969, in an effort to deal with the race question, he announced a new eight-week course to be taught by black students. "The Black Experience" included lectures and field trips. About 80 faculty members and students signed up.

By fall, a new Ethnic Studies curriculum, one of the student demands, had become a reality. But whereas eleven courses had been approved, only two appeared in the fall schedule of classes.

Fearful that the new program would exclusively cater to black students, one course was "Introduction to Ethnic Studies." This was a history of all people of color in the United States. Much to the dissatisfaction of campus African Americans, the second course was the "History of Brown and Red People in the United States." For the most part, blacks who had become extremely active in student activities since 1966, now completely withdrew.

In September 1969, *The San Matean* headlined: "The Agony and the Insanity—Will it Continue?"

Ewigleben resigned in December 1970 but continued in his position until March 1971.

American military involvement in Vietnam was a continual source of agitation on campus during the 1960s. Concerned students, most anti-war, conscientiously attended lectures and teach-ins.

Contributing to underlying stresses of the 1960s and 1970s was widespread student dissatisfaction about American participation in the war in Vietnam. Once more this placed them in direct confrontation with administrators, many of whom were decorated veterans of World War II and Korea.

In 1965, sensing that the college was becoming a haven for draft dodgers, Bortolazzo declared war on them. He informed trustees that enrollment was significantly higher than had been projected and that he suspected the increase was due to the draft. He pledged: "We will keep closer-then-ever track of our records this semester, and any one eligible for induction who fails to live up to our requirements will find himself reported to his draft board within 24 hours."

Instructors, many of whom shared the students' opposition to the war, were informed to scrupulously enforce attendance requirements. Instead, roll taking was often forgotten and there was noticeable grade inflation.

Discontented students growled about the government's introduction of the Selective Service Examination which was required if students were going to keep draft deferments. The test supposedly answered the question: "Do you have the skills to handle college?"

By 1967, sympathetic College of San Mateo counselors began offering advice on how students could be classified as conscientious objectors and presented a class entitled "The Selective Service System and What You Can Do About It."

Fiery anti-war historian Rudolph Lapp, himself a World War II veteran, in April 1967, led 50 CSM students to participate at Kezar Stadium in San Francisco's major anti-war protest to that time. An estimated 60,000 people took part.

Attitudes about the war weren't unanimous. Many on campus participated in Draft Resistance Week in April 1968. When student Bruce Peddy, organizer of the effort, called upon students to turn in their draft cards, he was struck in the face and knocked to the ground by a Vietnam veteran.

The next year, in October, CSM students crowded into the South Cafeteria to participate in the nationwide Vietnam Moratorium Day. They listened to Lapp and Congressman Pete McCloskey voice the feelings of the masses against the war. McCloskey received a standing ovation from students who had left classes—despite President Ewigleben's refusal to sanction the assembly.

The amphitheater in the fine arts complex of buildings and Washington Square (outside, east of the cafeteria) became the forums for debate on Vietnam.

The anti-war movement gathered momentum during the fall of 1969 when Vietnam veterans, hundreds of whom were now enrolled as students, came out in opposition to the struggle because of the "absurdity, violence and corruption" they'd seen there. By spring 1973, there were 1,300 veterans attending classes.

President Richard Nixon's ordered invasion of Cambodia in 1970, resulted in a coast-to-coast frenzy of student discontent. In San Mateo, at the request of the state governor, President Ewigleben canceled classes on May 7 and May 8. On the seventh, one of the largest crowds in college history heard speeches by historian Rudy Lapp, political science instructor Gregory Davis and other peace-demanding faculty and students. Ewigleben took to the podium to condemn the administration's action.

Lapp led a delegation of angry students to Washington, D.C., joining thousands of others from across the country who paraded the corridors of the Congressional Office Building demanding changes in U.S. policy.

George McGovern, an anti-war senator seeking the Democratic Party's nomination for president, swept onto the CSM campus June 2, 1972, to face an audience of between 3,000 and 4,000 students waiting in the college plaza. Introduced by David Mertes, CSM's new president, McGovern condemned Nixon and American involvement in the war.

U.S. Congressman Pete McCloskey addressed CSM students in April 1968 as part of Draft Resistance Week. He voiced the feeling of the masses who opposed the war.

Activism ebbed during the 1970s when students became increasingly convinced that the war in Vietnam was drawing to a close. Their energies were consumed by other matters. At least for a time, environmentalism became their cause.

While some continued to be involved in class boycotts and teach-ins regarding the war, others found themselves cleaning up the campus and rescuing local beaches from environmental disaster. Biology instructor John Williams, in March 1970, led a force of 200 students, faculty and administrators to combat an algae problem in Marina Lagoon (dividing Foster City from San Mateo).

President Richard M. Nixon's invasion of Cambodia in spring of 1970 generated one of the largest crowds in College of San Mateo's history.

Social science instructor Allen Weintraub created a new course, "Introduction to the Social and Natural Aspects of Ecology." Other such classes were added to the curriculum.

Robert Ewigleben, still CSM president in February 1970, opened an ecology conference on campus by declaring: "I hereby proclaim that College of San Mateo will be dedicated to the goal of human survival."

Vintage, a campus publication of the 1960s and 1970s, normally a hodge-podge of student creativity, devoted its 1970 edition to environmentalism. Editors noted that "man is faced with the extinction of the species which includes San Mateo County and the Bay Area as well as America."

On Earth Day, April 17, 1970, students proposed ridding the campus of all paper towel dispensers, replacing them with electric heating fans. They demanded use of bio-degradable soaps and the conversion of all campus vehicles to electric power.

Sexual stereotypes underwent careful scrutiny during the 1970s. In fall 1972, a woman police science major, Debbie Rondoni ('73), declaring that she didn't "agree with the classic role of the female as the homemaker," was elected student body president.

At the same time, Jeanie Higgins ('73) became editor of *The San Matean*. This was the first time that women had held these two important positions. Cartoons in the student newspaper which typically featured busty, empty-headed blonds almost immediately disappeared to be replaced by images of muscle-bound, air-headed men.

The presence of women was seen in all areas. They smashed sexual barriers, in 1973, in the previously all-male Athletics Department. Louise Glenn, a graduate of Mercy High School in Burlingame, became the first woman to join the swimming team; another woman won a spot on the tennis varsity. The student body election in January 1975, resulted in a run-off for president between a man and a woman—Frank Hunter ('75) and Jackie Massing. Massing triumphed with an amazing 62 percent of the votes. Dazed by his defeat, the wounded Hunter accused her of "special interest fanaticism."

By the 1980s, a breakdown of sexual stereotypes was seen on all parts of the campus. A woman in the fire science program is pictured maneuvering herself down from the library roof.

The San Matean mocked tradition in fall of 1972. "All you gorgeous guys can enter the 'Mr. CSM Student Body Beautiful Contest.'"

"Bodies, bodies and more bodies," headlined the newspaper when 14 hopeful contestants posted their photos in the cafeteria for student scrutiny.

More votes were cast for Mr. CSM than in the last Homecoming Queen contest and the previous student body election. The proud winners were Jack Schneider and Ray Irving. Both posed nude for photographers. One wore a Playboy-type bow tie and nothing else. The other, appearing more intellectual in glasses, was placed in front of a Viking ship statue.

The 1970s fad of "streaking," running through a crowd without clothes, made its CSM appearance in March 1974. Nick Satterlee, "CSM's first Naked Knight," stunned faculty and students when he rode along the campus mall on his Harley-Davidson. He was clad only in shoes and a crash helmet. Future streakers, both men and women, were eagerly anticipated. Rumors of expected appearances always spread rapidly, backed by scribbled announcements on blackboards and even restroom walls. Hundreds would congregate. One day, 11 streakers appeared within a single hour.

Attracting women 25 years of age and older to return to school became a priority of the 1970s. A Women's Re-entry Program was officially launched by dynamic English instructor Jane Hannigan in 1973. Twenty women enrolled in search of new educational beginnings. This program was one of the first such attempts in the United States. By 1980, amazingly successful, it boasted 110 students. Rose Marie Beuttler, a counselor specializing in returning women, commented that these women are "not over the hill, but on top of it."

Fourteen male students entered the 'Mr. CSM Body Beautiful Contest' in 1972. Thereafter, with increased emphasis on 'correctness,' the annual Spring Fever high jinks, held in May, featured more and more displays of masculine flesh. This Tongan dancer in 1991 (to use the language of an earlier era) was properly "scrutinized and appreciated."

It was in May 1971, that the College of San Mateo Music Department carved its place in annals of the institution. Jazz band conductor Dick Crest who joined the music faculty in 1958, led his musicians into a competition at the University of Illinois.

At the time the CSM Jazz Band was considered one of the seven best in the nation. In a recent competition, the group had triumphed over the

University of Southern California, the University of Nevada and California State University at Los Angeles.

The band was on a high when it arrived in Illinois. Within hours, the players were acclaimed as one of the top three jazz ensembles in the country.

Jazz was a proud part of the college's post World War II musical tradition. Elmer "Bud" Young, a talented and experienced musician who joined the department in 1946, liked to remark that at the time "jazz" was still considered a dirty word. Some thought teaching jazz was about as respectable as a college "offering a topless dancing class." Nevertheless, he started a stage jazz program as part of the college's regular music curriculum.

After World War II when most college music departments regarded "jazz" as a dirty word, San Mateo made it part of regular music curriculum. Trumpeter Fred Berry became the leader in 1984.

Only two other colleges in the nation included jazz in their music curriculum. To assure a good band, Young and Crest visited local high schools to recruit musicians. Almost immediately the band began to win awards and national recognition.

By the 1960s, few college organizations were more respectable or better known. The 20-piece band immediately won accolades. Under Dick Crest who took the baton from Young (and later trumpeter Fred Berry who joined the faculty in 1968), the group consistently vanquished rivals from both two-year and four-year colleges. Among its trophies are scores of first-place cups from the Marin Jazz Festival, the renowned Monterey Jazz Festival, the Pacific Coast Jazz Festival and numerous other competitions.

"College of San Mateo took pride in the 1960s and the 1970s as having one of the finest music departments in California," stated Leo Bardes, a faculty member beginning in 1965. "At one time we had a 100-voice day chorus, the largest in the state." Bardes, who later headed the department, conducted an 80-piece concert band and the 60-piece Bulldog Marching Band (formed by Dick Crest at Coyote Point in 1960). "Our theme song was 'Sons of San Mateo,'" recounted Bardes, reflecting on his band leading days.

In 1987, Bardes received an invitation from the U.S. Department of Labor to attend an all expenses paid five-day conference on Careers in Entertainment at Disney World in Florida. "I was surprised that only two community colleges in the nation were invited. All others were four-year institutions the likes of

Ohio State, the University of Texas and the University of Michigan."

During the spring of 1964, Frederic Roehr, the chorus director and head of the Music Department for almost 33 years, announced his retirement. Roehr recommended Galen Marshall, conductor of the choral program at San Francisco City College, as his replacement.

"It was a done deal when I got there," laughed the outgoing, gregarious Marshall, reflecting upon his brief interview with Julio Bortolazzo. Marshall began in fall 1964. Part of his assignment was to build a community chorus. With virtually no advanced publicity, he was surprised that twenty potential singers appeared the first night. By spring there were 100.

Thus began the Masterworks Chorale. The group grew to as many as 200 auditioned members. Singers came from as far away as Marin County, San Jose and Oakland. Marshall points out that his singers represented every walk of life. "We even have a couple of sex therapists." Two women sang with Masterworks for more than 30 years and quite a number sang for 20 years.

Beginning in 1964, Marshall conducted annual concerts in San Mateo and San Francisco. The group was normally accompanied by an orchestra of professional musicians. In addition to local concerts, Masterworks Chorale has made seven European tours. Singers, all registered college students, paid their own expenses.

In the Netherlands, at The Hague in 1973, the Masterworks Chorale, "almost as a lark," entered an international competition with 45 of the world's finest choruses. "We took first place…it was like being in the Olympics," recalled Marshall.

Since then, the group has sung to standing room only crowds wherever it has performed on the European continent. The group is perhaps better known there than in San Mateo.

In 1985, Marshall accepted an invitation from the People's Republic of China for Masterworks to sing in the First Annual Festival of American Music at Shanghai. The maestro, who accompanied 60 singers to China, remembered the two-and-a-half week China tour as a high point in his career. "Culturally it was a magnificent experience. We were treated like absolute royalty by the Chinese."

Maestro Galen Marshall, founder of CSM's Masterworks Chorale.

The China trip became indelibly etched in the memories of the singers who participated. The group, which specialized in traditional sacred and secular choral masterpieces by major composers, sang primarily American folk songs and Negro spirituals including "Yankee Doodle," "Dem Bones" and "Camptown Races."

College of San Mateo public relations officer Georgi La Berge, who accompanied the singers, recalled that "the heat in China was staggering and many were overcome by it." After one concert, Marshall complained that he "could wring the sweat from my tails and vest."

Nevertheless, China was a special experience. La Berge reflected on the concert sung in Beijing. "Most in the audience were drably dressed and quite reserved...but when the chorus sang 'Dem Bones,' the crowd perked up and began to move."

On April 30, 1989, Marshall conducted his singers in Verdi's *Requiem* at Carnegie Hall in New York City. Peter Tiboris, music director of the Manhattan Philharmonic Orchestra, declared that Marshall's 208-voice chorus sang "without question...one of the greatest performances of Verdi's *Requiem* in this hall." The 1,800 people in attendance gave the Masterworks Chorale a standing ovation.

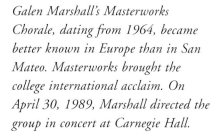

Galen Marshall's Masterworks Chorale, dating from 1964, became better known in Europe than in San Mateo. Masterworks brought the college international acclaim. On April 30, 1989, Marshall directed the group in concert at Carnegie Hall.

College of San Mateo's dominating personality during the late 1970s and throughout the next decade was Lois A. Callahan. The Missouri born woman's rise to academic prominence was meteoric. She earned a master's degree at Chico State College and a doctorate in education from the University of Southern California. Few success stories compare.

Callahan joined the faculty as a business instructor in 1968. That she was a trailblazer and comfortably navigated uncharted professional territory became almost immediately apparent.

She became successful in the male-dominated milieu of college administration. After a mere four years at CSM she was named director of cooperative education. Then, in 1974, she became the first woman dean of occupations at San Jose City College.

On April 1, 1976, Callahan returned to San Mateo as dean of instruction, the highest ranking administrative post ever held by a woman in the 54-year history of the institution. Upon the resignation of David Mertes in 1978, Callahan was named CSM's acting president, a position which became permanent in May 1979.

This was "in an era when 'Dress for Success' meant a gray suit and a pair of trousers featuring a front fly, not a tailored skirt with a side placket," remarked Linda Scholer, president of College of San Mateo's Academic Senate in 1991.

Confidantes agreed that both as a person and a colleague Callahan was warm and caring; many admitted, however, that these qualities were never fully appreciated by some on the faculty. Many saw her only in public meetings and determined from her countenance that she was cool and aloof. Nevertheless, those who worked closely with Callahan during her 13 years in the position found her capable, effective and an extremely hard worker.

Unlike some predecessors who relied heavily on staff, she enjoyed being involved in projects and actually doing things herself. Perhaps no president has ever been such a master of detail. Win Smith, an associate dean, added that Callahan was "amazingly fair" and "always was willing to take full responsibilities for her actions."

Lois A. Callahan became College of San Mateo's first woman president in 1979. Associates noted that she was a hands-on administrator, capable of keeping track of both the big picture and the most minute details as well. She was appointed Chancellor of the San Mateo County Community College District in 1991.

KCSM-TV began broadcasting from College Heights after the erection of its antenna and tower near the library in 1964.

This president wasn't one to become involved in public disagreement; she was no grandstander. Weeks went by that neither her name nor photograph appeared in *The San Matean.* Her administrative style was quiet, effective and relatively simple. She would determine what she thought was right for College of San Mateo and, having done so, was steadfastly unwilling to compromise. She made the place work.

Callahan was devoted to the concept of KCSM-TV and the whole principle of educational television. When she became president, the station, which traced its history back to the opening of College Heights, was in difficult straits. The station's equipment, much of it antiquated, had been neglected and KCSM still broadcast in black and white. It seemed apparent that the station was going to close. "KCSM was an asset we were going to lose," she remarked, reflecting on the situation.

She choreographed an exchange between Channel 14, College of San Mateo, and Channel 60, a San Francisco Spanish-speaking language station, KDTV. Management at that station desired the lower number on the dial and was willing to make a trade. College of San Mateo got both a new transmitter and color capability. The exchange, completed in 1979 and 1980, brought KCSM into the modern era. The station went from 13,800 to 1.5 million watts. "We realized that our place on the dial would not be as easily accessible as Channel 14," remarked Callahan. "On the other hand it seemed to me at the time that as an educational station if people couldn't find Channel 60 they probably were not going to benefit from our offerings." KCSM became one of the last stations in the country to convert to color.

For a decade before she became president, the need for a child care center had been an on-going theme. A number of off-campus locations were surveyed as possible sites for a center. In 1975, student body president Jackie Massing led a group of 200 interested students to a meeting of college trustees to pressure them into creating a child care facility. Trustees were willing to do everything possible to support the concept, except pay for it.

Shortly after becoming acting president, Callahan learned that the Ralph Lazarus family of Cincinnati had contacted the college about the possibility of creating some kind of memorial for their daughter Mary Meta Lazarus who had died after a brief illness at the age of 37. She had studied art at College of San Mateo for three semesters. Her father, Ralph Lazarus, was chairman of the board for Federated Department Stores, parent company of Bullock's, I. Magnin and other stores. Earlier, the Lazarus family had approached the CSM administration about building a memorial for their daughter. They felt that college officials had not responded enthusiastically to their ideas.

Callahan intervened. She met with the family on several occasions. They spoke of creating a scholarship program for re-entry women or possibly supporting a child care facility. Though badly needed, the latter suggestion was wrought with possible controversy. Trustees did not regard child care as a college responsibility. A basic change in philosophy was required.

The Lazarus family visited San Mateo in early 1978, receiving a tour of the campus from Callahan. Ultimately they made an offer of $500,000 for the creation of a child care center. This was accepted by trustees on Oct. 10, 1979. A site for the 5,000 square foot center was chosen in a park-like area on the northeast side of the campus overlooking San Francisco Bay. The family remained friends of the college and subsequently created an endowment fund to support the facility.

The Mary Meta Lazarus Child Care Center was dedicated May 1, 1981, with a ribbon cutting by Trustee Eleanore D. Nettle and Ralph Lazarus. It opened in September 1981.

English professor Michael Kimball, for many years a Callahan assistant, admired her ability to immediately recognize and zero in on the heart of problems and solve them. In that regard, "Dr. Callahan is as capable as any administrator I've ever known," he stated.

Political science professor Gregory Davis, who did not always agree with Callahan, noted admiringly that unlike some others in top positions, she had a real political sense of dealing with the faculty. "Callahan fully understood the collegial nature of a college."

Callahan's executive leadership was recognized well beyond the borders of San Mateo. In 1985 she prepared a report revealing the dismal condition of

During the 1970s, a campus child care facility became a goal of students and administrators. In 1979, trustees accepted a gift of $500,000 for construction of the Mary Meta Lazarus Child Care Center at College Heights. Lois Callahan and Trustee Eleanore D. Nettle broke ground for the center.

119

equipment at College of San Mateo and dozens of other community colleges in California. This report was instrumental in convincing then Governor George Deukmejian to approve $31 million in the state funding for college equipment needs. In 1989, as part of a University of Texas study, she was honored by other community college presidents as an outstanding leader.

"She was very action oriented," added Peter Landsberger, who succeeded Callahan in 1992. She was named Chancellor of the three college San Mateo County Community College District in 1991.

Callahan kept sight of her objectives. "She always has one more critical task to add to the list," stated Landsberger. "She can acknowledge one moment that a person has his or her plate very full and that we need to set priorities. But five minutes later she has identified two or three more things that need to be accomplished and worked on right away.

"As a result, those who *don't* know her well are likely to find her all business, real no nonsense, a genuine taskmaster. But those who know her soon find out that she is always concerned about people's feelings and essential needs and marvelously tolerant of their foibles and their eccentricities…She treats people with fairness and respect," Landsberger concluded.

For all its streamlined architectural elegance, College Heights was a nightmarish obstacle course for handicapped and physically impaired students. Every day was a new challenge not experienced by the physically fit for whom the college had been designed. John Warnecke drew his plans in an era before consideration was given to people with physical disabilities.

For the disabled, every curb might as well have been an insurmountable obstacle. Artistic slopes were agonizing if not impossible ordeals. Classroom buildings were like prisons.

Late in the 1980s, a wheelchair ramp was finally installed from the bus stop up to the level of the buildings. Only after it had been completed, however, was it discovered that it was ineffective. The ramp was too steep for safety and the railings were too high.

Handicapped parking places were usually too narrow and often built on inclines.

Bathroom stalls weren't up to code.

For the first 30 years of College Heights, classes taught on the second floors were completely inaccessible. If disabled students requested an upstairs class they were denied the right to enroll if there was another instructor teaching the same course on the ground floor. If no other section was available, the entire class was moved. Only in 1991 did President Callahan succeed in getting almost half a million dollars for the installation of elevators in classroom buildings.

Even the Administration Building was originally constructed without an elevator. When handicapped students wished to consult with counselors (whose offices were upstairs), they were required to telephone first and counselors would come downstairs. They met in hallways.

Disabled students claimed their academic needs were not being met.

The College Health Center, staffed by a nurse, was located on the second floor of the Administration Building, at the top of a long twisting stairway.

Longtime administrator Philip Morse explained the reason for this unique situation. The building was designed so that the rear would be against a hillside with direct access to the second floor via a ramp.

But, during construction, dirt was needed for fill at another part of the campus. Thus, without authorization, the hill behind the building was cut away, leaving a free-standing structure. Health and other vital services were stranded on the second floor. Finally, but not until 20 years after the campus opened, this was remedied when an elevator was installed. The cost of the construction was almost $90,000.

The elegant library, centerpiece of the campus, was especially inhospitable for the disabled who were required to gain access through a dark and cluttered service entrance and the freight elevator. In 1980, Bill Hare, a disabled student, asked trustees to have an elevator installed in the library. He was told that an elevator would "ruin the aesthetics" of the building. Shelves were too high to be reached. Rows between shelves were too narrow for wheelchairs.

Administrator Philip D. Morse joined the faculty as a business instructor in 1940 when the college was still at Baldwin. He later served in a variety of administrative posts and retired in 1981.

Whereas the earthquake of Oct. 17, 1989, caused almost no campus damage, the temblor sent chills racing along the spines of administrators. Seismic experts took a long look at the concrete and glass library and declared it a disaster waiting to happen.

Plans, including removal of asbestos, were immediately undertaken to reinforce the structure, create handicapped accessibility through construction of ramps and installation of an elevator, and to improve utilization of the overall space.

Books and equipment were removed to temporary buildings for storage and the library was closed, 1995-1996. The first phase of the remodeling was accomplished by fall 1996, at a cost of $3.9 million. A further $8.7 million remodeling was planned.

College Heights was designed and constructed in accordance with established codes, standards and practices, but after the 1989 jolt, these almost 30-year old standards were considered technically obsolete and inadequate.

Seismic engineers recommended the immediate reinforcement of the colonnades connecting various buildings throughout the campus. Reconstruction of these colonnades, architectural signatures of College Heights, was undertaken at a cost of $490,584.

There was one single day in the history of College of San Mateo, May 17, 1980, when its football gridiron was dedicated as an airfield by the Federal Aviation Authority. Aircraft above the peninsula, heading for San Francisco International Airport, were rerouted.

Since the days of Jum Morris when the college introduced its first aviation course, aeronautics had played a significant role in the life of the institution. May 17 was the only air show ever staged on the campus.

Sounding like "giant gnats," gliders swooped over the crowd watching from the grandstand and soared above the stadium. Helicopters from Fort Ord flew across at tree-top level. A large troop carrying helicopter hovered 200 feet above the field and participants were treated to a demonstration by U.S.

Marines repelling to the ground. Later in the day the helicopters landed on the field to permit tours by students.

Because of CSM's reputation for its vocational programs and the high quality of its overall curriculum, along with its close proximity to Stanford and the University of California, the U.S. State Department added College of San Mateo to its list of places to visit for foreign dignitaries. During the 1980s, a series of distinguished leaders arrived in San Mateo.

On June 18, 1980, Lois Callahan hosted an 11-member delegation of educators from the People's Republic of China. The Chinese received an explanation of California's sprawling community college system. Delegates toured the campus.

The State Department book on how these visitors were to be treated "was almost six inches thick…it included everything, even what they would eat," stated Callahan. A light meal of pastries (from Chantilly Lace Bakery in San Mateo), California strawberries, Jasmine tea, Farmer's Coffee and Minute Maid Orange Juice was served. There were no substitutions.

A more relaxed visitation came in October 1982, when the State Department arranged a tour for Ferenc Ratkai, Deputy Minister of Culture and Education of Hungary. No special instructions preceded him. Ratkai, staying in San Francisco, came to San Mateo on the commuter train, alone, and rode a San Mateo Transit bus to College Heights. After the visit, a sympathetic Callahan drove him back to his hotel.

Security officers were atop buildings surveying the campus with binoculars on Oct. 1, 1980, when Republican vice presidential hopeful George Bush and wife Barbara arrived to be greeted by the press, demonstrators and the CSM Jazz Band.

Lois Callahan was particularly taken with the graciousness of Barbara Bush but noted that, before he spoke, the very precise Mrs. Bush took her aside to instruct Callahan on just how her husband was to be introduced.

Following his talk and a question session with students, despite blistering heat, Bush decided on running the campus par course. English Professor Mike Kimball accompanied Bush, other faculty members, a handful of students and

Following a speech on campus in October 1980, vice presidential candidate George Bush led instructors, students and reporters on a circuit of the exercise course.

Secret Service agents. Kimball accidently brushed against Bush's arm and was himself instantly struck with a breath-stopping body block thrown by a beefy Secret Service agent who barked: "Never touch the candidate." The three miles were covered in 22 minutes.

While Bush sweated in the heat, President Callahan fretted about whether or not there was soap and clean towels in the men's locker room. (Years later, Bush's photograph, snapped when he was jogging during a state visit in Budapest, appeared on the cover of a Hungarian magazine. He was wearing the CSM T-shirt given to him in 1980.)

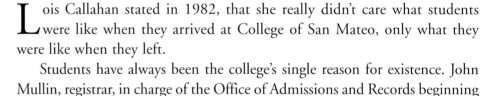

Lois Callahan stated in 1982, that she really didn't care what students were like when they arrived at College of San Mateo, only what they were like when they left.

Students have always been the college's single reason for existence. John Mullin, registrar, in charge of the Office of Admissions and Records beginning in 1984, stared blankly when queried about the number of students who have attended classes since 1922. The number was so enormous, it was almost inconceivable. He noted that in the period between 1975 and 1981, approximately 435,000 individuals finished studies at the college.

Almost nostalgically, former students from Coyote Point and College Heights remembered the days before the advent of the computer when registration lines snaked around corners and extended, seemingly for blocks. Admissions officers still regard the early delays with amazement. "It took students hours," recalled Joanne Dunbar. "Many new friendships were made," added Gretchen Crusick. At the absolute best of times, an hour in the registration line was usual; at worst, three to five hours or even longer wasn't uncommon. Phyllis Hechim ('64), an administrative assistant, recalled that some of the greatest nightmares occurred in the early days of computers when the electronic devices refused to function.

Indelibly etched in the memories of students, who attended College of San Mateo in the era before computers and telephone registration, were the long registration lines which at times snaked across the campus for blocks. Some stood in line for hours.

Unlike many colleges, no attempt was ever made to create an alumni association or, for that matter, keep track of either graduates or fellow travelers who simply attended a few classes. Suffice it to say, however, that after 75 years, it is difficult to identify the family along the San Francisco Peninsula, which has not been represented at the college by at least one member.

For thousands, College of San Mateo has been a springboard to success. Raymond Daba ('35) was the son of an Italian immigrant grocer. He received hes bachelor's and a law degree from Stanford, sat on the State Board of Education and was one of the county's most prominent attorneys. Ed Bauer ('30) was the longtime publisher-editor of the *Half Moon Bay Review*. Raymond Hemming ('39), graduated from Stanford and received a commission in the Navy during World War II. He became a decorated admiral in the U.S. Naval Reserve in addition to being the founder of Hemming Morse, the largest accounting firm in Northern California.

Earle Marsh ('32) graduated from the University of California and McGill Medical School in Montreal. He spent a career as a gynecologist and psychiatrist. He helped draft the original Kinsey Report. Irene Simpson Neasham ('36) was director of the History Room at Wells Fargo Bank in San Francisco. Kenneth L. Fisher started as a student (at age 16) during the 1960s, but flunked out. He returned a year later and went on to become one of the nation's top investment advisors.

The college left an imprint on the radio-television industry. Bonnie Chastain ('73), carved a niche as a broadcaster and the first woman engineer in the Columbia Broadcasting System. Jon Miller ('71), hired by the Oakland A's baseball team as the play-by-play announcer, was the youngest in the history of major league baseball. He went on to become the voice of the Baltimore Orioles and the weekly game announcer for the ESPN television network.

KCSM-TV personality Claire Mack ('74) began courses at the college in 1968. One day she wandered into the office of station manager Doug Montgomery, to proclaim: "Make me a broadcaster." She went to work for KCSM almost immediately and became

Claire Mack ('74) studied broadcasting at CSM. She worked for both KCSM radio and television. She interviewed presidential hopeful Jesse Jackson during a campaign stop in San Mateo, spring 1984.

Rosemary Phipps Pfeiffer ('67) became the first woman elected to the San Mateo County Superior Court bench.

the station's best known personality. She involved herself in local politics and was elected to the city council and was San Mateo's first black mayor. Her on-camera career spanned three decades.

Louis B. Dematteis began his education at San Mateo Junior College during the 1920s. He was named San Mateo County District Attorney in 1949 and five years later was appointed to a seat on the Superior Court bench, the first Italian-American to fill either position. Rosemary Phipps Pfeiffer ('67), recipient of the College of San Mateo Distinguished Alumni Award (1995), was the first county woman elected to the Superior Court.

Police officer Mark J. Raffaelli ('69), became South San Francisco Chief of Police in 1993. Bruce Cumming, somewhat confused as a student, developed enthusiasm for education after enrolling in police science courses at CSM. He pinned on the chief's star at Menlo Park in 1988. Michael Parker, named Millbrae chief in 1992, began law enforcement work at College of San Mateo during the 1960s. Captain James Baker, during the 1990s, was Area Commander for the California Highway Patrol in Redwood City, and took his first police course at College Heights in 1965. So many police officers of all ranks attended the college that police science graduates came to dominate the local law enforcement community.

Richard Fischer ('62), elected both Freshmen and Sophomore president, left his mark as a private investigator. Few have equalled his professional record. He investigated 25 murder cases and provided evidence for the acquittals of eight defendants.

Leon Fletcher ('41), who studied at San Mateo Junior College with the longtime speech and drama instructor Ada Beverage, taught at Monterey Peninsula College while writing three books and publishing more than 500 magazine articles on the art of public speaking.

A number of ethnic minorities who participated in the College Readiness Program between 1966 and 1968, were the first in their families to attend college and the first who were not on welfare. Albert Nelson went on to Berkeley and became an architect for the U.S. Navy. Michelle Mouton, one of the original group, received a bachelor's degree and teaching credential;

she is an elementary school teacher in East Palo Alto. Charles Franklin became a hospital administrator.

Super Bowl winning coaches and broadcasters Bill Walsh of the San Francisco Forty Niners and John Madden of the Oakland Raiders, were Bulldogs and played on the College of San Mateo gridiron during the 1950s. Running back Bill Ring ('79), played with the champion Forty Niners (1981-1986). He majored in business and felt "prepared academically in all areas." He graduated from Brigham Young University.

John Noce ('51), a member of the San Mateo County Sports Hall of Fame, began coaching baseball at CSM in 1962. To his credit are 700 plus wins, more community college baseball victories than any coach in California. Two hundred-five of his players went on to four-year institutions, 135 with scholarships. Ninety-three signed with professional teams, eight were on big league rosters. Fifty-two of Noce's players accepted coaching positions after leaving CSM. Noce also served as the coach for the Italian Baseball Federation. He coached Italian baseball teams at the Olympics in Los Angeles, Barcelona and Atlanta.

High on the college's list of outstanding sportsmen was Greg Buckingham, named "Athlete of the Year" in 1965 by *The San Matean*. Swimming coach Rich Donner remembered that as soon as Buckingham jumped into the pool he began assaulting junior college records.

During one semester, Buckingham became holder of the 100, 200 and 500 freestyle, 100 backstroke, 200 breaststroke, 200 butterfly and 200 individual medley school marks. His pool records included the 100, 200 and 500 free, 100 backstroke and 200 individual medley.

In 1968, after leaving CSM, Buckingham joined the U.S. Olympic team and swam in the oxygen-thin atmosphere of Mexico City. He took a Silver Medal in the individual medley.

Buckingham's younger brother Lindsey enrolled at CSM. Coach Donner, hoping for another phenomenon, encouraged him to try out for swimming. Lindsey told Donner he wanted to devote his energies to music. Donner tried to dissuade him, assuring the young man that there was no future in music.

John Madden wore the uniform of a Bulldog before going on to fame as coach of the Oakland Raiders and a television sports announcer.

Coach John Noce ('51) became legendary in baseball circles as the community college coach with the most wins in California history.

Leslie A. Williams graduated with the Class of 1939. He was a pilot during World War II, performed as a dancer and became a successful San Mateo attorney.

Years later, Buckingham, then a member of Fleetwood Mac, sent Donner a photo of himself with his Rolls Royce.

College of San Mateo has produced a crop of writers. Willa Okker Iverson ('24) was the top local reporter for the Associated Press and author of best-seller *The Strange Case of Constance Flood*. Jack Bluth ('49) and Ken Costa ('69) were sports and business editors respectively of the *San Mateo Times*. Paul Scanlon ('65) became senior editor for *Rolling Stone Magazine*.

Winthrop Griffith ('51), once the editor of *The San Matean*, graduated from Stanford where he had been editor of the *Stanford Daily*. He later commented that the instruction he received while at San Mateo was "as good or better than anything I got at Stanford." Griffith went to Washington and, during the 1960s, served as press secretary to Minnesota Senator Hubert H. Humphrey. Thereafter, Griffith became successful as a free-lance writer. Among his published works were *Humphrey: A Candid Biography*.

Gregory L. Vistica, a student during the 1980s, twice nominated for the Pulitzer Prize and winner of numerous local and national awards for investigative reporting, became involved in national security matters in 1982. As a *Newsweek* correspondent, he covered the intelligence community. He was responsible for exposing the Navy's Tailhook sex-abuse scandal. His reporting forced the Navy to initiate widespread investigations leading to historic changes in the military. Vistica wrote the book *Fall from Glory: The Men Who Sank the U.S. Navy*.

San Mateo attorney Leslie A. Williams ('39), a pilot during World War II, initially achieved fame as a dancer. Television producer and performer Merv Griffin, a native of San Mateo, attended the college. He completed no units and, after getting into trouble with the administration, was asked to leave. Dana Carvey was more successful. He later performed in the movie "Wayne's World" and was one of the regular crew on the popular television program "Saturday Night Live." Paul Albert Marianette ('51) went to Hollywood where he starred (under the name Paul Mantee) in "Robinson Crusoe on Mars" and in several television series including episodes "Hawaii 5-0" and "Cagney & Lacey." Musician Cal Tjader attended CSM. Phil Lesh ('71) was a drummer with the Grateful Dead. Carolyn Stoner ('71) became "Miss California."

College of San Mateo hasn't been for everyone. During the fall of 1962, Jerome (Jerry) Garcia, founder of the Grateful Dead, dropped out after attending just three class meetings.

San Mateo Junior College produced a number of war heroes. Japanese-American Kenji Kato attended the jaysee for a time before enlisting in the service just before Pearl Harbor. He spent three years in the Pacific. When he returned, his chest glistened with three Bronze Stars denoting the Northern Solomon, New Guinea and Philippines campaigns. He also wore the Philippines Liberation Ribbon with a Bronze Star and Bronze Arrowhead for taking part in the initial landing with assault troops at Bougainville.

Kato translated intercepted Japanese messages. He instructed Marines in the ways of Japanese soldiers and interrogated prisoners of war.

He was reunited with his family in San Mateo in 1945. A mother, father and two sisters were released early from the Topaz Relocation Center in Utah, where they had been interned, to participate in his homecoming.

Actor Paul Mantee starred in the movie "Robinson Crusoe on Mars" and a number of different television programs.

James Swett, a soccer player who left San Mateo Junior College to serve his country, returned a national hero. As a Marine Corps pilot, he electrified America with his daring. In one amazing 15-minute engagement, in April 1943, he blasted seven Japanese bombers from the skies above the Solomon Islands. Before completing his tour, the 24-year old Capt. Swett shot down a total of 16 enemy planes.

Additionally he flew 53 missions against Japan's inner defensive positions and several over Tokyo. He destroyed 11 planes on the ground and sank nine small cargo boats in Tokyo harbor.

Swett was decorated with the Distinguished Flying Cross, the Air Medal with oak leaf clusters, the Purple Heart and, the nation's highest military decoration, the Medal of Honor.

Thomas W. Mellen ('38) joined the Army as an enlisted man in 1941. He went through Officers Candidate School and was commissioned in June 1942. He received decorations in World War II, Korea and Vietnam. In 1972, promoted to major general, he assumed command of the 25th

129

Infantry Division in Hawaii. He retired in 1974.

College of San Mateo graduates experienced a share of both bad and good wartime fortune. Andrew Boyer ('34) joined the Naval Reserve as a radio man in 1940. He was aboard the battleship *USS Nevada* Dec. 7, 1941, at Pearl Harbor. The *Nevada* was the only battleship which survived the initial attack and managed to get underway. Pounced on by Japanese planes, the great ship was torpedoed and bombed. Badly damaged, she had to be beached. Thereafter, Boyer was assigned to the aircraft carrier *USS Lexington*. In the spring of 1942, *Lexington* was attacked and sunk during the battle of the Coral Sea. Boyer emerged from both encounters unscathed.

J. Craig Venter ('70) became a medical doctor and founder and president of The Institute for Genomic Research, established in 1992 with a 10-year, $70 million grant. The institute, according to Venter, was devoted to accelerating the sequencing of human, animal and plant genomes to better understand the role that genes and gene products played in development, evolution, physiology and disease. This institute was one of the largest non-commercial facilities in the world devoted to large scale DNA sequencing and bioinformatics.

Since 1963, the Little Theater has been the setting for opening day of the year faculty meetings.

A number of graduates returned to accept teaching and counseling positions at the college. Among those (on the faculty during the seventy-fifth anniversary year) included Sylvia Aguirre ('77), Kathryn "Kitty" Brown ('72) and Steven Morehouse ('71) all of whom became counselors. Elaine Burns ('72) created the Career Center. Gregg Atkins ('69) took over the college library. James Petromilli (electronics), Roberta Reynolds (English), Dennis Stack (drafting) and Kenneth Kennedy (political science) taught in their respective fields. Gary Dilley ('68) became Dean of Athletics and Physical Education.

Though not a graduate of College of San Mateo, Counselor Modesta Garcia, a native of Texas, attended between 1972 and 1975 and was a product of the College Readiness Program. She was counseled by Adrian Orozco who played an important part in her life, becoming her first Mexican-American role model. Garcia, who went on to receive a master's degree in education from Harvard and held several teaching positions in the East, returned in 1987 to CSM's Multi-Cultural Center. She became a counselor in 1989.

Wini Stetson counseling a student in her office at Coyote Point.

One student who carved her name in the history of the institution was Winifred (Wini) Stetson ('38) who enrolled in fall of 1936. Within a short period of time, she was employed in the Co-op or bookstore. Later she served as bookstore manager and the secretary for student affairs. During the 1950s, she resigned after major differences of philosophy with President Elon Hildreth.

Stetson took time to complete a bachelor's degree at San Francisco State College. She reapplied to San Mateo for a job and was hired to teach typing and shorthand. She recalled that her interview with Julio Bortolazzo was "electrifying." Upon completion of her master's degree in psychology, Stetson joined the counseling faculty. She retired in 1977.

In a category all of his own was Ed Roberts, paralyzed from the neck down by polio as a freshman at Burlingame High School. He was confined to an iron lung. Roberts learned to breath by using the muscles in his neck. He reached a point when he could breath independently for one hour a day. During that hour, because of his desire for an education, through sheer guts and determination, he attended class in an automated wheelchair at College of San Mateo's Coyote Point campus.

Spring Fever, a week just for fun in May, before final examinations, was always highlighted by rubber boat races in the campus reflecting pool.

For countless thousands, College of San Mateo has spelled opportunity and been a springboard to successful careers.

"I knew I could make it intellectually, but it was at CSM I found I could make it physically," he stated later. Roberts became the first severely disabled student to attend the University of California.

He ultimately liberated himself from the iron lung for 14 hours a day. In 1976, the year Roberts won the Junior College Association Alumni Award, California Governor Jerry Brown appointed him to head the State Department of Rehabilitation. He led 2,300 employees and managed a $90 million annual budget. Many societal improvements for the severely disabled, including state regulations for ramps and elevators were the result of Roberts' efforts. He died in 1995. He was 59.

Attempting to highlight all of College of San Mateo's outstanding graduates is an impossible and dangerous undertaking. Were the authors to continue writing, many would come forth with additional lists of names and events which had been overlooked. This survey is a brief sampling that does *not* even attempt to come close to being definitive.

Furthermore, the urge to begin identifying prominent faculty personalities, while challenging, was an impulse authors managed to resist. Such would have become an absolutely impossible chore. There have been so many. Suffice it to say that for 75 years faculty efforts have opened great new vistas for countless thousands of students.

Class Act represents the efforts of administrators, faculty and students. Most of the photographs used covering the period from the 1960s to the 1990s were taken by CSM photographer Isago Tanaka.

The authors especially wish to thank members of College of San Mateo's classified staff—the administrative assistants, secretaries, clerks, switchboard operators, grounds keepers and cafeteria personnel—the true unsung heroes of the institution. It was their cooperation and willingness to dig deeply into files, storage bins and the recesses of their minds to resurrect long forgotten tales which allowed us to reconstruct the personality of the college.

The success of this book is to everyone's credit.